Favorite Brand Name

GIFTS FROM THE

Christmas

KITCHEN

PUBLICATIONS INTERNATIONAL, LTD.

Front cover photography: Sanders Studio, Inc., Chicago

Pictured on the front cover *(clockwise from top right):* Cherry Eggnog Quick Bread *(page 170)*, Cookies and Cream Cheesecake Bonbons *(page 319)*, Chocolate Reindeer *(page 202)*, Crispy Thumbprint Cookies *(page 244)*, Chocolate-Dipped Orange Logs *(page 221)*, Triple Layer Chocolate Mints *(page 290)*, Cracked Peppercorn Honey Mustard *(page 54)*, Soft Pretzels *(page 42)* and Raspberry Vinegar *(page 57)*.

Pictured on the contents page *(clockwise from top right):* Peanut Butter Fudge *(page 286)*, Dark Chocolate Fudge *(page 286)* and Traditional Peanut Brittle *(page 345)*.

Pictured on the back cover *(clockwise from top left):* Cranberry-Orange Snack Mix *(page 8)*, Cranberry Cheesecake Muffins *(page 174)* and Cranberry-Apple Relish *(page 82)*.

Microwave Cooking: Microwave ovens vary in wattage. Use the cooking times as guidelines and check for doneness before adding more time.

CONTENTS

GIFT GIVING TIPS

Unwrapping a homemade present in a beautifully hand-crafted package is one of life's greatest pleasures. *Gifts from the Christmas Kitchen* makes creating these special gifts easier than ever. Each recipe has detailed preparation steps and many have full-color photographs illustrating innovative packaging ideas. Delight your family and friends by giving the most meaningful gift of all—one crafted by hand that's from the heart.

THE PERFECT PACKAGE

Homemade gifts are made extraordinary when tucked into unique packages lavished with decorative accessories. Craft, stationery and kitchen supply stores carry a wide variety of supplies that can add a special touch to your gifts.

BASKETS: These versatile hold-alls are available in a wide variety of materials and sizes. Large, sturdy ones are well suited for packing entire gift themes. Oblong shapes are wonderful for breads and smaller versions are just right for cookies.

BOTTLES: Assorted airtight bottles etched with decorative patterns are perfect for barbecue sauces. Always choose securely stoppered bottles to help prevent any leakage.

BOXES: Boxes come in a variety of shapes and sizes and are well suited for cookies, candies, snack mixes and truffles. Large boxes are perfect for packing entire gift themes.

GIFT BAGS: These handy totes come in a variety of sizes. Pack individual cookies and caramels in smaller bags, and goodie-filled bottles, jars and canisters in larger bags.

GLASS JARS: Jars are perfect for packing mustards and snack mixes. Be sure to pack more perishable items, such as sauces, chutneys and jams, in jars with airtight lids.

TINS: Metal containers with tight-fitting lids are just the right thing for snack mixes, cookies and candies because they hold up well when sent through the mail.

FINISHING TOUCHES

After the goodies are made and tucked into decorative packages, you are ready to put the finishing touches on your gift.

CELLOPHANE: Cellophane is an indispensable material for hard-to-wrap gifts such as plates of food, individual breads and candies. Gather the ends and secure with satiny ribbons for a pretty finish.

DECORATIVE PAPERS: Papers come in a variety of finishes, including glossy and metallic, and many can be enhanced with rubber stamps. Colorful tissue papers are perfect for tucking into gift boxes and bags.

GIFT TAGS: Assorted metal and paper tags come in handy when making personalized notes and cards for your gifts. They also make great labels for storing directions.

RIBBONS, SATIN CORDS AND STRINGS: Thick colorful ribbons, metallic strings and thin shiny cords are perfect accents for homemade wrapping papers.

RUBBER STAMPS AND INK PADS: Stamps with holiday or food themes paired with colorful inks are perfect for decorating plain papers or wrapping and making personalized note cards for recipes, labels for sauces and jams, storing directions and gift tags.

SPECIAL INSTRUCTIONS

Before you give your gifts, did you remember to include:

Storage directions? They are included at the end of most recipes and it's a good idea to include them with your gifts. Storage directions are an absolute must for perishable items and those that must be held in the refrigerator.

Serving notes and suggestions? Valuable serving tips are included at the end of some of the recipes, and many photographs illustrate innovative serving suggestions and uses for your edible gifts.

SHIPPING GIFTS
General Instructions

When sending edible holiday gifts, proper food selection and packaging is important. Moist quick breads and sturdy cookies are ideal choices as are many non-fragile confections, such as fudge and caramels. It is best to prepare foods just before packing and mailing, and to choose a speedy method of shipment. Foods should be completely cooled before packing. Wrap all breakable containers in bubble wrap and fill boxes with packing peanuts.

Don't Let the Cookies Crumble!

Soft, moist cookies can survive packing and shipping better than fragile, brittle cookies. Brownies and bar cookies generally pack well but avoid those with moist fillings and frostings since they tend to become sticky at room temperature. Wrap each type of cookie separately to retain flavors and textures. Pack wrapped cookies in rows as tightly as possible to prevent breakage during shipping.

CHOCOLATE TECHNIQUES
Melting Chocolate

Make sure the utensils used for melting chocolate are completely dry. Moisture will cause the chocolate to "seize," meaning it will become stiff and grainy. If this happens, add ½ teaspoon shortening (not butter) for each ounce of chocolate and stir until smooth. Chocolate will scorch easily, and once scorched cannot be used. Use one of the three following methods for successful melting:

DOUBLE BOILER: This is the safest method because it prevents scorching. Place the chocolate in the top of a double boiler or in a heatproof bowl over hot, not boiling water; stir chocolate until smooth. (Make sure that the water remains just below a simmer and is one inch below the bottom of the top pan.) Be careful that no steam or water gets into the chocolate.

DIRECT HEAT: Place the chocolate in a heavy saucepan and melt over very low heat, stirring constantly. Remove the chocolate from heat as soon as it is melted. Be sure to watch the chocolate carefully because it scorches easily.

MICROWAVE OVEN: Place an unwrapped 1-ounce square or 1 cup of chips in a small microwavable bowl. Microwave on HIGH 1 to 1½ minutes, stirring after 1 minute. Stir the chocolate at 30-second intervals until smooth. Be sure to stir microwaved chocolate since it may retain its original shape even when melted.

Tempering Chocolate

Melted real chocolate must go through a process of cooling and heating called tempering to avoid blooming. You'll need a candy thermometer for this process. Here's how to temper chocolate:

1. Cover an ordinary heating pad with a towel; place on countertop. Turn the pad to its lowest setting.

2. Grate or finely chop chocolate. Place ¾ of chocolate in the top of a double boiler. Melt over hot, not boiling, water. Stir until chocolate melts.

3. Attach candy thermometer to side of pan, making sure bulb is submerged in chocolate but not touching bottom of pan. Chocolate should be between 110° and 120°F. (Do not let chocolate heat above 120°F.)

4. Remove top of double boiler, being careful not to let steam from bottom of double boiler get near chocolate, and place on towel-covered heating pad. Turn heating pad off. Add remaining ¼ chocolate, 1 tablespoon at a time, stirring gently until it melts. Stir until chocolate has cooled to between 86° and 90°F.

5. The chocolate is now ready for dipping. Check the temperature of the chocolate regularly as you stir and dip. Adjust the temperature of the chocolate by turning the heating pad on and off momentarily. The chocolate's temperature should remain between 86° and 90°F.

Note: If the chocolate rises above 92°F, the temper will be lost and you must begin again.

THE "SKINNY" ON BUTTER

Many of the recipes in this book specifically call for butter. Do not assume that butter, margarine and low-fat spreads are interchangeable. The fat content of margarines and low-fat spreads varies greatly from brand to brand. Margarine has slightly less fat than butter and an oilier base. Some spreads are up to 50% water and may contain gums. Substituting these products in a recipe that specifically calls for butter will alter the taste and texture of the finished product. Ensure successful holiday baking by using the ingredients called for in the recipe.

SENSATIONAL SEASONAL SNACKS

CRANBERRY-ORANGE SNACK MIX

2 cups oatmeal cereal squares
2 cups corn cereal squares
2 cups mini pretzels
1 cup whole almonds
¼ cup butter
⅓ cup frozen orange juice concentrate, thawed
3 tablespoons packed brown sugar
1 teaspoon ground cinnamon
¾ teaspoon ground ginger
¼ teaspoon ground nutmeg
⅔ cup dried cranberries

1. Preheat oven to 250°F. Spray 13×9-inch baking pan with nonstick cooking spray.

2. Combine cereal squares, pretzels and almonds in large bowl; set aside.

3. Melt butter in medium microwavable bowl on HIGH 45 to 60 seconds. Stir in orange juice concentrate, brown sugar, cinnamon, ginger and nutmeg until blended. Pour over cereal mixture; stir well to coat. Place in prepared pan and spread to one layer.

4. Bake 50 minutes, stirring every 10 minutes. Stir in cranberries. Let cool in pan on wire rack, leaving uncovered until mixture is crisp. Store in airtight container or resealable plastic food storage bag. *Makes 8 cups*

Cranberry-Orange Snack Mix

Santa Fe Trail Mix

1½ cups pecan halves
1 cup cashews
¾ cup roasted shelled pistachio nuts
½ cup pine nuts
⅓ cup roasted sunflower seeds
3 tablespoons butter
2½ teaspoons ground cumin
¼ teaspoon garlic powder
¼ cup plus 1 tablespoon chili sauce
1 chipotle chile in adobo sauce, about 3 inches long*
1 tablespoon frozen orange juice concentrate, thawed
Cooking spray
1 tablespoon dried cilantro, divided

*Chipotle chile peppers are smoked jalapeño peppers and commonly available canned in adobo sauce.

1. Preheat oven to 300°F. Line 14×11-inch baking sheet with foil; set aside.

2. Combine pecans, cashews, pistachios, pine nuts and sunflower seeds in large bowl.

3. Combine butter, cumin and garlic powder in small microwavable bowl. Microwave on HIGH 45 to 50 seconds or until butter is melted and foamy; stir to blend.

4. Place butter mixture, chili sauce, chipotle chile and orange juice concentrate in food processor or blender; process until smooth. Pour sauce over nut mixture; stir to coat evenly. Spread mixture in single layer on prepared baking sheet.

5. Bake about 1 hour, stirring every 10 minutes. Remove from oven and spray mixture evenly with cooking spray. Sprinkle 1½ teaspoons cilantro over mixture. Stir mixture with spatula and repeat with additional cooking spray and remaining cilantro. Set baking sheet on wire rack to cool. Leave uncovered at least 1 hour before storing in airtight container or resealable plastic food storage bag. *Makes 4 cups*

Santa Fe Trail Mix

Sun-Dried Tomato Pizza Snack Mix

2 cups wheat cereal squares

2 cups unsweetened puffed corn cereal

2 cups puffed rice cereal

2 cups mini cheese crackers

1 cup roasted sunflower seeds

3 tablespoons grated Parmesan cheese

3 tablespoons butter

2 tablespoons olive oil

2 teaspoons dried Italian seasoning

1½ teaspoons garlic powder

¼ cup tomato sauce

1 teaspoon balsamic vinegar

⅜ teaspoon sugar

⅛ teaspoon salt

8 to 9 sun-dried tomatoes packed in oil, diced

1. Preheat oven to 250°F. Spray 13×9-inch baking pan with nonstick cooking spray.

2. Combine cereal squares, puffed corn, puffed rice, cheese crackers and sunflower seeds in large bowl; set aside.

3. Combine cheese, butter, oil, Italian seasoning and garlic powder in medium bowl. Microwave on HIGH 1 to 1½ minutes until foamy and herbs release their aromas. Stir in tomato sauce, vinegar, sugar and salt. Pour over cereal mixture; stir well to coat. Place in prepared pan and spread to one layer.

4. Bake 55 to 60 minutes, stirring every 15 minutes. Stir in sun-dried tomatoes 15 minutes before finished baking. Let cool in pan set on wire rack about 2 hours, leaving uncovered until mixture is crisp and tomato pieces have lost their moisture. Store in airtight container or resealable plastic food storage bag.

Makes 7 cups

Sun-Dried Tomato Pizza Snack Mix

13

MEXICALI CRUNCH

4 cups corn flakes
2 quarts popped corn
3 cups corn or tortilla chips
1 cup roasted peanuts
½ cup Mazola® Margarine
½ cup KARO® Light or Dark Corn Syrup
¼ cup packed brown sugar
1 package (1.25 ounces) taco seasoning mix

1. Preheat oven to 250°F. In large roasting pan combine corn flakes, popped corn, corn chips and peanuts.

2. In medium saucepan combine margarine, corn syrup, brown sugar and taco seasoning. Bring to boil over medium heat, stirring constantly. Pour over corn flake mixture; toss to coat well.

3. Bake 60 minutes, stirring every 15 minutes. Cool, stirring frequently. Store in tightly covered container.

Makes about 4 quarts

Variation: For a Texicali version of this spicy snack, substitute 5 tablespoons of chili seasoning mix for the taco seasoning.

Microwave Directions: In large roasting pan combine corn flakes, popped corn, corn chips and peanuts. In 1-quart microwavable bowl combine margarine, corn syrup, brown sugar and taco seasoning. Microwave on HIGH (100%), 2 to 4 minutes or until mixture boils, stirring once. Pour over corn flake mixture; toss to coat well. Bake as directed.

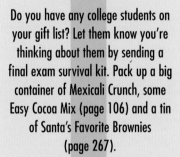

Do you have any college students on your gift list? Let them know you're thinking about them by sending a final exam survival kit. Pack up a big container of Mexicali Crunch, some Easy Cocoa Mix (page 106) and a tin of Santa's Favorite Brownies (page 267).

TAKE-ALONG SNACK MIX

1 tablespoon butter or margarine
2 tablespoons honey
1 cup toasted oat cereal, any flavor
½ cup coarsely broken pecans
½ cup thin pretzel sticks, broken in half
½ cup raisins
1 cup "M&M's"® Chocolate Mini Baking Bits

In large heavy skillet over low heat, melt butter; add honey until blended. Add cereal, nuts, pretzels and raisins, stirring until all pieces are evenly coated. Continue cooking over low heat about 10 minutes, stirring frequently. Remove from heat; immediately spread on waxed paper until cool. Add "M&M's"® Chocolate Mini Baking Bits. Store in tightly covered container.   *Makes about 3½ cups*

PEPPY SNACK MIX

3 plain rice cakes, broken into bite-size pieces
1½ cups bite-size frosted shredded wheat biscuit cereal
¾ cup pretzel sticks, halved
3 tablespoons reduced-calorie margarine, melted
2 teaspoons low-sodium Worcestershire sauce
¾ teaspoon chili powder
⅛ to ¼ teaspoon ground red pepper

Preheat oven to 300°F. Combine rice cakes, wheat cereal and pretzels in 13×9-inch baking pan. Combine margarine, Worcestershire sauce, chili powder and pepper in small bowl. Drizzle over cereal mixture; toss to combine. Bake, uncovered, 20 minutes, stirring after 10 minutes.
Makes 6 servings

Caramel-Cinnamon Snack Mix

CARAMEL-CINNAMON SNACK MIX

2 tablespoons vegetable oil
½ cup popcorn kernels
½ teaspoon salt, divided
**1½ cups packed light brown
    sugar**
½ cup butter or margarine
½ cup corn syrup
**¼ cup red hot cinnamon
    candies**
**2 cups cinnamon-flavored
    shaped graham crackers**
**1 cup red and green candy-
    coated chocolate pieces**

A big tin of Caramel-Cinnamon Snack Mix will let your co-workers know that you appreciated all their hard work throughout the year!

1. Grease 2 large baking pans; set aside.

2. Heat oil in large saucepan over high heat until hot. Add corn kernels. Cover pan. Shake pan constantly over heat until kernels no longer pop. Divide popcorn evenly between 2 large bowls. Add ¼ teaspoon salt to each bowl; toss to coat. Set aside.

3. Preheat oven to 250°F. Combine sugar, butter and corn syrup in medium saucepan. Cook over medium heat until sugar melts, stirring constantly with wooden spoon. Bring mixture to a boil. Boil 5 minutes, stirring frequently.

4. Remove ½ of sugar mixture (about ¾ cup) from saucepan; pour over 1 portion of popcorn. Toss with lightly greased spatula until evenly coated.

5. Add red hot candies to saucepan. Stir constantly with wooden spoon until melted. Pour over remaining portion of popcorn; toss with lightly greased spatula until evenly coated.

6. Spread each portion of popcorn in even layer in separate prepared pans with lightly greased spatula.

7. Bake 1 hour, stirring every 15 minutes with wooden spoon to prevent popcorn from sticking together. Cool completely in pans. Combine popcorn, graham crackers and chocolate pieces in large bowl. Store in airtight container at room temperature up to 1 week. *Makes about 4 quarts*

SWEET AND SPICY SNACK MIX

6 cups popped corn
3 cups miniature pretzels
1½ cups pecan halves
⅔ cup packed brown sugar
⅓ cup butter or margarine
1 teaspoon ground cinnamon
¼ teaspoon ground red pepper

1. Combine popped corn, pretzels and nuts in large bowl.

2. Place brown sugar, butter, cinnamon and red pepper in 2-cup microwavable cup. Microwave at HIGH 1½ minutes or until bubbly.

3. Pour butter mixture over popcorn mixture; toss with rubber spatula until well mixed. *Makes about 10 cups*

CINNAMON APPLE CHIPS

2 cups unsweetened apple juice
1 cinnamon stick
2 Washington Red Delicious apples

1. In large skillet or saucepan, combine apple juice and cinnamon stick; bring to a low boil while preparing apples.

2. With paring knife, slice off ½ inch from top and bottom of apples and discard (or eat). Stand apples on either cut end; cut crosswise into ⅛-inch-thick slices, rotating apple as necessary to cut even slices.

3. Drop slices into boiling juice; cook 4 to 5 minutes or until slices appear translucent and lightly golden. Meanwhile, preheat oven to 250°F.

4. With slotted spatula, remove apple slices from juice and pat dry. Arrange slices on wire racks, being sure none overlap. Place racks on middle shelf in oven; bake 30 to 40 minutes until slices are lightly browned and almost dry to touch. Let chips cool on racks completely before storing in airtight container. *Makes about 40 chips*

Tip: There is no need to core apples because boiling in juice for several minutes softens core and removes seeds.

Favorite recipe from **Washington Apple Commission**

Sweet and Spicy Snack Mix

FRUITED GRANOLA

3 cups uncooked quick-cooking oats
1 cup sliced unblanched almonds
1 cup honey
3 tablespoons butter or margarine, melted
½ cup wheat germ or honey wheat germ
1 teaspoon ground cinnamon
3 cups whole grain or whole wheat cereal flakes
½ cup dried blueberries or golden raisins
½ cup dried cranberries or tart cherries
½ cup dried banana chips or chopped pitted dates

1. Preheat oven to 325°F. Spread oats and almonds in single layer in 13×9-inch baking pan. Bake 15 minutes or until lightly toasted, stirring frequently with wooden spoon. Remove pan from oven. Set aside.

2. Combine honey, butter, wheat germ and cinnamon in large bowl until well blended. Add oats and almonds; toss to coat completely. Spread mixture in single layer in baking pan.

3. Bake 20 minutes or until golden brown. Cool completely in pan on wire rack. Break mixture into chunks with wooden spoon.

4. Combine oat chunks, cereal, blueberries, cranberries and banana chips in large bowl.

5. Store in airtight container at room temperature up to 2 weeks. *Makes about 10 cups*

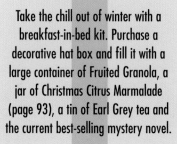

Take the chill out of winter with a breakfast-in-bed kit. Purchase a decorative hat box and fill it with a large container of Fruited Granola, a jar of Christmas Citrus Marmalade (page 93), a tin of Earl Grey tea and the current best-selling mystery novel.

Fruited Granola

Praline Pecans & Cranberries

3½ cups pecan halves
¼ cup light corn syrup
¼ cup packed light brown sugar
2 tablespoons butter or margarine
1 teaspoon vanilla
¼ teaspoon baking soda
1½ cups dried cranberries or cherries

1. Preheat oven to 250°F. Grease 13×9-inch baking pan. Set aside. Cover large baking sheet with heavy-duty aluminum foil. Set aside.

2. Spread pecans in single layer in prepared baking pan.

3. Combine corn syrup, sugar and butter in small microwavable bowl. Microwave at HIGH 1 minute. Stir. Microwave 30 seconds to 1 minute or until boiling rapidly. Stir in vanilla and baking soda until well blended. Drizzle evenly over pecans; stir with wooden spoon until evenly coated.

4. Bake 1 hour, stirring every 20 minutes with wooden spoon. Immediately transfer mixture to prepared baking sheet, spreading pecans evenly over foil with lightly greased spatula.

5. Cool completely. Break pecans apart with wooden spoon. Combine pecans and cranberries in large bowl.

6. Store in airtight container at room temperature up to 2 weeks. *Makes about 5 cups*

Peppered Pecans

3 tablespoons butter or margarine
3 cloves garlic, minced
1½ teaspoons TABASCO® pepper sauce
½ teaspoon salt
3 cups pecan halves

Preheat oven to 250°F. In small skillet, melt butter. Add garlic, TABASCO® sauce and salt; cook 1 minute. Toss pecans with butter mixture; spread in single layer on baking sheet. Bake 1 hour or until pecans are crisp, stirring occasionally.

Makes 3 cups

Praline Pecans & Cranberries

CITRUS CANDIED NUTS

1 egg white
1½ cups whole almonds
1½ cups pecan halves
1 cup powdered sugar
2 tablespoons lemon juice
2 teaspoons grated orange peel
1 teaspoon grated lemon peel
⅛ teaspoon ground nutmeg

Preheat oven to 300°F. Generously grease 15½×10½×1-inch jelly-roll pan. Beat egg white in medium bowl with electric mixer on high speed until soft peaks form. Add almonds and pecans; stir until coated. Stir in powdered sugar, lemon juice, orange peel, lemon peel and nutmeg. Turn out onto prepared pan, spreading nuts in single layer.

Bake 30 minutes, stirring after 20 minutes. Turn off oven. Let nuts stand in oven 15 minutes more. Immediately remove nuts from pan to sheet of foil. Cool completely. Store up to 2 weeks in airtight container. *Makes about 3 cups*

SPICED SUGARED NUTS

MAZOLA NO STICK®
Cooking Spray
2 cups pecans, walnuts or peanuts
1 cup sugar
⅓ cup water
¼ cup KARO® Light Corn Syrup
1 teaspoon cinnamon
¼ teaspoon ground allspice
¼ teaspoon salt
1 teaspoon vanilla

1. Spray 13×9×2-inch baking pan with cooking spray. Add nuts. Place in 250°F oven while preparing coating.

2. In 2-quart saucepan combine sugar, water, corn syrup, cinnamon, allspice and salt. Stirring constantly, bring to boil over medium heat. Stirring occasionally, cook until temperature on candy thermometer reaches 236°F or until a small amount of mixture dropped into very cold water forms a soft ball which flattens on removal. Remove from heat.

3. Add nuts and vanilla. Stir until nuts are completely coated.

4. Return nuts to baking pan. Working quickly with 2 forks, separate nuts into individual pieces. Cool completely. Store in airtight container. *Makes about 1 pound*

Candied Rum Walnuts: *Follow recipe for Spiced Sugared Nuts. Use walnuts. Omit cinnamon, allspice and vanilla. Add 1 teaspoon rum extract with walnuts.*

Top to bottom: Citrus Candied Nuts and Elegant Cream Cheese Mints (page 370)

Deviled Mixed Nuts

3 tablespoons vegetable oil
2 cups assorted unsalted nuts, such as peanuts, almonds, Brazil nuts or walnuts
2 tablespoons sugar
1 teaspoon paprika
½ teaspoon chili powder
½ teaspoon curry powder
½ teaspoon ground cumin
½ teaspoon ground coriander
½ teaspoon black pepper
¼ teaspoon salt

Heat oil in large skillet over medium heat; cook and stir nuts in hot oil 2 to 3 minutes or until browned. Combine remaining ingredients in small bowl; sprinkle over nuts. Stir to coat evenly. Heat 1 to 2 minutes more. Drain nuts on wire rack lined with paper towels.   *Makes 2 cups*

Barbecued Peanuts

2 tablespoons butter or margarine, melted
¼ cup barbecue sauce
¾ teaspoon garlic salt
⅛ teaspoon ground red pepper*
1 jar (16 ounces) dry roasted lightly salted peanuts

*For Spicy Barbecued Peanuts, increase ground red pepper to ¼ teaspoon.

1. Preheat oven to 325°F. Grease 13×9-inch baking pan. Set aside.

2. Whisk melted butter, barbecue sauce, garlic salt and pepper in medium bowl until well blended. Add peanuts; toss until evenly coated.

3. Spread peanuts in single layer in prepared baking pan.

4. Bake 20 to 22 minutes or until peanuts are glazed, stirring occasionally. Cool completely in pan on wire rack, stirring occasionally to prevent peanuts from sticking together.

5. Spoon into decorative tin; cover. Store at room temperature up to 2 weeks.   *Makes about 4 cups*

Left to right: Cheese Twists (page 36) and Deviled Mixed Nuts

Harvest-Time Popcorn

2 tablespoons vegetable oil
1 cup popcorn kernels
2 cans (1¾ ounces each) shoestring potatoes (3 cups)
1 cup salted mixed nuts or peanuts
¼ cup margarine, melted
1 teaspoon dill weed
1 teaspoon Worcestershire sauce
½ teaspoon lemon-pepper seasoning
¼ teaspoon garlic powder
¼ teaspoon onion salt

1. Heat oil in 4-quart saucepan over high heat until hot. Add popcorn kernels. Cover pan; shake continuously over heat until popping stops. Popcorn should measure 2 quarts. Do not add butter or salt.

2. Preheat oven to 325°F. Combine popcorn, shoestring potatoes and nuts in large roasting pan. Set aside.

3. Combine margarine, dill, Worcestershire sauce, lemon-pepper seasoning, garlic powder and onion salt in small bowl.

4. Pour evenly over popcorn mixture, stirring until evenly coated.

5. Bake 8 to 10 minutes, stirring once. Let stand at room temperature until cool. Store in airtight containers.

Makes 2½ quarts

Easy Caramel Popcorn

MAZOLA NO STICK® Cooking Spray
3 quarts popped popcorn
3 cups unsalted mixed nuts
1 cup packed brown sugar
½ cup KARO® Light or Dark Corn Syrup
½ cup (1 stick) MAZOLA® Margarine or butter
½ teaspoon salt
½ teaspoon vanilla
½ teaspoon baking soda

1. Spray large shallow roasting pan with cooking spray. Combine popcorn and nuts in pan; place in 250°F oven while preparing glaze.

2. In heavy 2-quart saucepan combine brown sugar, corn syrup, margarine and salt. Stirring constantly, bring to boil over medium heat. Without stirring, boil 5 minutes. Remove from heat; stir in vanilla and baking soda. Pour syrup mixture over warm popcorn and nuts, stirring to coat.

3. Bake in 250°F oven 60 minutes, stirring occasionally. Remove from oven. Cool; break apart. Store in tightly covered container.

Makes about 4 quarts

Harvest-Time Popcorn

POPCORN CRUNCHIES

12 cups popped corn (about
¾ cup unpopped)
1½ cups sugar
⅓ cup water
⅓ cup corn syrup
2 tablespoons butter or
margarine
1 teaspoon vanilla

Preheat oven to 250°F. Grease large shallow roasting pan. Add popcorn. Keep warm in oven while making caramel mixture.

Place sugar, water and corn syrup in heavy 2-quart saucepan. Stir over low heat until sugar has dissolved and mixture comes to a boil. Carefully clip candy thermometer to side of pan (do not let bulb touch bottom of pan). Cook over low heat without stirring about 10 minutes or until thermometer registers 280°F. Occasionally wash down any sugar crystals that form on side of the pan using pastry brush dipped in warm water. Immediately remove from heat. Stir in butter and vanilla until smooth.

Pour hot syrup mixture slowly over warm popcorn, turning to coat kernels evenly. Set aside until cool enough to handle but warm enough to shape. Butter hands. Working quickly, lightly press warm mixture into 2-inch balls. Cool completely. Store in airtight container.   *Makes about 14 popcorn balls*

Create your own snack-attack gift bag. Line a holiday gift bag with colorful tissue paper and fill it with Popcorn Crunchies, a jar of Cracked Peppercorn Honey Mustard (page 54) and a tin of Soft Pretzels (page 42) for the ideal homespun gift for all your neighbors.

Popcorn Crunchies

Cinnamon REDHOT® Popcorn

10 cups air-popped popcorn (½ cup unpopped)
1½ cups (7 ounces) coarsely chopped pecans
¾ cup granulated sugar
¾ cup packed light brown sugar
½ cup light corn syrup
3 tablespoons FRANK'S® Original REDHOT® Cayenne Pepper Sauce
2 tablespoons honey
6 tablespoons (¾ stick) unsalted butter, room temperature, cut into thin pats
1 tablespoon ground cinnamon

1. Preheat oven to 250°F. Place popcorn and pecans in 5-quart ovenproof bowl or Dutch oven. Bake 15 minutes.

2. Combine sugars, corn syrup, RedHot® sauce and honey in 2-quart saucepan. Bring to a full boil over medium-high heat, stirring just until sugars dissolve. Boil about 6 to 8 minutes or until soft crack stage (290°F on candy thermometer). Do not stir. Remove from heat.

3. Gradually add butter and cinnamon to sugar mixture, stirring gently until well blended. Pour over popcorn, tossing to coat evenly.* Spread popcorn mixture on greased baking sheets, using two forks. Cool completely. Break into bite-size pieces. Store in airtight container up to 2 weeks.

Makes 18 cups

If popcorn mixture sets too quickly, return to oven to re-warm. Popcorn mixture may be shaped into 3-inch balls while warm, if desired.

Cinnamon REDHOT® Popcorn

Cheesy Sun Crisps

**2 cups (8 ounces) shredded
Cheddar cheese**
**½ cup grated Parmesan
cheese**
**½ cup sunflower oil
margarine, softened**
3 tablespoons water
1 cup all-purpose flour
¼ teaspoon salt (optional)
1 cup uncooked quick oats
**⅔ cup roasted, salted
sunflower seeds**

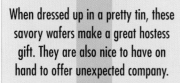

When dressed up in a pretty tin, these savory wafers make a great hostess gift. They are also nice to have on hand to offer unexpected company.

Beat cheeses, margarine and water in bowl until blended. Mix in flour and salt. Stir in oats and sunflower seeds until combined. Shape into 12-inch-long roll; wrap securely. Refrigerate about 4 hours or up to 1 week.

Preheat oven to 400°F. Lightly grease cookie sheets. Cut roll into ⅛- to ¼-inch slices; flatten each slice slightly. Place on prepared cookie sheets. Bake 8 to 10 minutes or until edges are light golden brown. Remove immediately; cool on wire rack.   *Makes 4 to 5 dozen crackers*

Favorite recipe from **National Sunflower Association**

Cheesy Sun Crisps

CHEESE TWISTS

1 cup all-purpose flour
½ teaspoon baking soda
½ teaspoon dry mustard
½ teaspoon salt
⅛ teaspoon ground red pepper
¾ cup grated Parmesan
    cheese, divided
½ cup butter or margarine,
    softened
3 egg yolks
2 teaspoons water
1 egg white, slightly beaten
1 tablespoon sesame seeds
    (optional)

Preheat oven to 400°F. Grease two cookie sheets. Combine flour, baking soda, mustard, salt and red pepper in large bowl. Reserve 1 tablespoon cheese; stir remaining cheese into flour mixture. Cut in butter with pastry blender or 2 knives until mixture resembles fine crumbs. Add egg yolks and water, mixing until dough forms. Shape into a ball; flatten and wrap in plastic wrap. Refrigerate 2 hours or until firm.

Roll out dough on lightly floured surface into 12-inch square (about ⅛ inch thick). Brush surface lightly with egg white and sprinkle with remaining 1 tablespoon cheese and sesame seeds, if desired. Cut dough in half. Cut each half crosswise into ¼-inch strips. Twist 2 strips together. Repeat with remaining strips. Place 1 inch apart on prepared cookie sheets.

Bake 6 to 8 minutes or until light golden brown. Remove from cookie sheets and cool completely on wire racks. Store in airtight container. *Makes about 48 twists*

Pizza Bread Sticks

1 package (¼ ounce) active dry yeast
¾ cup warm water (105°F to 115°F)
2½ cups all-purpose flour
½ cup (2 ounces) shredded part-skim mozzarella cheese
¼ cup (1 ounce) shredded Parmesan cheese
¼ cup chopped red bell pepper
1 green onion with top, sliced
1 medium clove garlic, minced
½ teaspoon dried basil leaves
½ teaspoon dried oregano leaves
¼ teaspoon red pepper flakes (optional)
¼ teaspoon salt
1 tablespoon olive oil

1. Preheat oven to 400°F. Spray 2 large nonstick baking sheets with nonstick cooking spray; set aside.

2. Sprinkle yeast over warm water in small bowl; stir until yeast dissolves. Let stand 5 minutes or until bubbly.

3. Meanwhile, place all remaining ingredients except oil in food processor; process a few seconds to combine. With food processor running, gradually add yeast mixture and oil. Process just until mixture forms a ball. (Add an additional 2 tablespoons flour if dough is too sticky.)

4. Transfer dough to lightly floured surface; knead 1 minute. Let dough rest 5 minutes. Roll out dough with lightly floured rolling pin to form 14×8-inch rectangle; cut dough crosswise into ½-inch-wide strips. Twist dough strips; place on prepared baking sheets.

5. Bake 14 to 16 minutes or until lightly browned.

Makes 14 servings

Bran and Honey Rye Breadsticks

BRAN AND HONEY RYE BREADSTICKS

1 package (¼ ounce) active
    dry yeast
1 teaspoon sugar
1½ cups warm water (110°F)
3¾ cups all-purpose flour,
    divided
1 tablespoon honey
1 tablespoon vegetable oil
½ teaspoon salt
1 cup rye flour
½ cup whole bran cereal
    Skim milk

1. Dissolve yeast and sugar in warm water in large bowl. Let stand 10 minutes. Add 1 cup all-purpose flour, honey, oil and salt. Beat with electric mixer at medium speed 3 minutes. Stir in rye flour, bran cereal and additional 2 cups all-purpose flour or enough to make moderately stiff dough.

2. Knead dough on lightly floured surface 10 minutes or until smooth and elastic, adding remaining ¾ cup all-purpose flour as necessary to prevent sticking. Place in greased bowl; turn over to grease surface. Cover with damp cloth; let rise in warm place 40 to 45 minutes or until doubled in bulk.

3. Spray 2 baking sheets with nonstick cooking spray. Punch dough down. Divide into 24 equal pieces on lightly floured surface. Roll each piece into an 8-inch rope. Place on prepared baking sheets. Cover with damp cloth; let rise in warm place 30 to 35 minutes or until doubled in bulk.

4. Preheat oven to 375°F. Brush breadsticks with milk. Bake 18 to 20 minutes or until breadsticks are golden brown. Remove from baking sheets. Cool on wire racks.

Makes 24 breadsticks

CRISPY RANCH BREADSTICKS

**2 tablespoons dry ranch party
dip mix
2 tablespoons sour cream
1 package (10 ounces)
refrigerated pizza dough
Butter, melted**

1. Preheat oven to 400°F. Combine dip mix and sour cream in small bowl; set aside.

2. Unroll pizza dough on lightly floured work surface. Shape dough into 16×10-inch rectangle. Brush with melted butter. Spread dip mixture evenly over top of dough; cut into 24 (10-inch) strips. Shape into desired shapes.

3. Place breadsticks, ½ inch apart, on parchment-lined or well-greased baking sheets. Bake 10 minutes or until golden brown. Serve immediately or place on wire rack to cool.

Makes 24 breadsticks

Crispy Spiced Nut Breadsticks: Place 1 cup chopped pecans and 1 tablespoon vegetable oil in plastic bag; toss to coat. Combine ¼ teaspoon chili powder, ¼ teaspoon ground cumin, ¼ teaspoon curry powder, ⅛ teaspoon ground cinnamon and a dash of ground red pepper in small bowl. Add to nuts; toss to coat. Place nuts in small pan over medium heat and stir constantly until nuts are lightly toasted. Sprinkle nut mixture with 1 teaspoon garlic salt; cool to room temperature. Instead of spreading dough with sour cream mixture, sprinkle ½ cup very finely chopped spiced nuts over dough (store remaining nuts in tightly covered container). Cut into 24 (10-inch) strips. Shape into desired shapes. Bake as directed.

Top to bottom: Crispy Spiced Nut Breadsticks and Crispy Ranch Breadsticks

Soft Pretzels

1¼ cups milk
    4 to 4½ cups all-purpose
        flour, divided
    ¼ cup sugar
    1 package active dry yeast
    1 teaspoon baking powder
    1 teaspoon garlic salt
    ½ cup unsalted butter, melted
    2 quarts water
    2 tablespoons baking soda
        Coarse salt, sesame seeds,
            or poppy seeds

1. Heat milk in small saucepan over low heat until temperature reaches 120°F to 130°F.

2. Combine 3 cups flour, sugar, yeast, baking powder and garlic salt in large bowl. Add milk and butter. Beat vigorously 2 minutes. Add remaining flour, ¼ cup at a time, until dough begins to pull away from sides of bowl.

3. Turn out dough onto lightly floured surface; flatten slightly. Knead 10 minutes or until smooth and elastic, adding flour if necessary to prevent sticking.

4. Shape dough into ball. Place in large lightly oiled bowl; turn dough over once to oil surface. Cover with towel; let rise in warm place about 30 minutes.

5. Divide dough into 18 equal pieces. Roll each piece into 22-inch-long rope on lightly oiled surface. Form the rope into a "U" shape. About 2 inches from each end, cross the dough. Cross a second time. Fold the loose ends up to the rounded part of the "U"; press the ends to seal. Turn the pretzels over so that the ends are on the underside and reshape if necessary. Cover with towel; let rest 20 minutes.

6. Preheat oven to 400°F. Fill a large Dutch oven ¾ full with water. Bring to a boil over high heat. Add baking soda. Carefully drop pretzels, 3 at a time, into boiling water for 10 seconds. Remove with slotted spoon. Place on parchment-lined or well-greased baking sheets. Sprinkle with coarse salt, sesame seeds or poppy seeds.

7. Bake 15 minutes or until golden brown. Place on wire rack.   *Makes 18 large pretzels*

Soft Pretzels

SESAME-ONION TWISTS

2 tablespoons butter or margarine
1½ cups finely chopped onions
¼ teaspoon paprika
Nonstick cooking spray
1 loaf (16 ounces) frozen bread dough, thawed
1 egg, beaten
1 tablespoon sesame seeds

1. Grease large baking sheet; set aside. Melt butter in medium skillet over medium heat until foamy. Add onions and paprika; cook until onions are tender, stirring occasionally. Remove from heat.

2. Spray work surface with nonstick cooking spray. Roll thawed bread dough into 14×12-inch rectangle.

3. Spread onion mixture on one side of dough. Fold dough over onion mixture to make 14×6-inch rectangle.

4. Pinch 14-inch side of dough to seal. Cut dough into 14 lengthwise strips.

5. Gently twist dough strip two times and place on prepared sheet. Press both ends of strip down on cookie sheet. Repeat with remaining strips.

6. Cover with towel. Let twists rise in warm place about 40 minutes or until doubled in bulk. Brush with egg; sprinkle with sesame seeds.

7. Preheat oven to 375°F. Bake 15 to 18 minutes or until golden brown.   *Makes 14 twists*

Sesame-Onion Twists

SOUTHWESTERN SNACK SQUARES

1¼ cups all-purpose flour
1 cup thinly sliced green onions
¾ cup QUAKER® Enriched Corn Meal
1 tablespoon brown sugar
2 teaspoons baking powder
1 teaspoon dried oregano
½ teaspoon ground cumin
¼ teaspoon salt (optional)
1 cup milk
¼ cup vegetable oil
1 egg
1 cup (4 ounces) shredded Cheddar cheese
1 can (4 ounces) chopped green chilies
¼ cup finely chopped red bell pepper
2 sliced crisp-cooked bacon, crumbled

Preheat oven to 400°F. Grease 11×7-inch baking dish.

Combine flour, green onions, corn meal, brown sugar, baking powder, oregano, cumin and salt in large bowl; mix well. Combine milk, oil and egg in small bowl. Add to corn meal mixture; mix just until moistened. Spread evenly into prepared dish. Combine cheese, chilies, pepper and bacon in medium-size bowl. Sprinkle evenly over corn meal mixture.

Bake 25 to 30 minutes or until wooden toothpick inserted into center comes out clean. Let stand 10 minutes before cutting.

Makes about 15 appetizers

Southwestern Snack Squares

Greek Spinach-Cheese Rolls

1 loaf (1 pound) frozen bread dough
1 package (10 ounces) frozen chopped spinach, thawed and squeezed dry
¾ cup (3 ounces) crumbled feta cheese
½ cup (2 ounces) shredded reduced-fat Monterey Jack cheese
4 green onions, thinly sliced
1 teaspoon dried dill weed
½ teaspoon garlic powder
½ teaspoon black pepper

1. Thaw bread dough according to package directions. Spray 15 muffin cups with nonstick cooking spray; set aside. Roll out dough on lightly floured surface to 15×9-inch rectangle. (If dough is springy and difficult to roll, cover with plastic wrap and let rest 5 minutes to relax.) Position dough so long edge runs parallel to edge of work surface.

2. Combine spinach, cheeses, green onions, dill weed, garlic powder and pepper in large bowl; mix well.

3. Sprinkle spinach mixture evenly over dough to within 1 inch of long edges. Starting at long edge, roll up snugly, pinching seam closed. Place seam side down; cut roll with serrated knife into 1-inch-wide slices. Place slices cut sides up in prepared muffin cups. Cover with plastic wrap; let stand 30 minutes in warm place until rolls are slightly puffy.

4. Preheat oven to 375°F. Bake 20 to 25 minutes or until golden. Serve warm or at room temperature. Rolls can be stored in refrigerator in airtight container up to 2 days.

Makes 15 servings (1 roll each)

Greek Spinach-Cheese Rolls

ANTIPASTO CRESCENT BITES

2 ounces cream cheese (do not use reduced fat or fat-free cream cheese)

1 package (8 ounces) refrigerated crescent roll dough

1 egg plus 1 tablespoon water, beaten

4 strips roasted red pepper, cut into 3×¾-inch strips

2 large marinated artichoke hearts, cut in half lengthwise to ¾-inch width

1 thin slice Genoa or other salami, cut into 4 strips

4 small stuffed green olives, cut in half

1. Preheat oven to 375°F. Cut cream cheese into 16 equal pieces, about 1 teaspoon per piece; set aside.

2. Remove dough from package. Unroll on lightly floured surface. Cut each triangle of dough in half to form 2 triangles. Brush outer edges of triangle lightly with beaten egg.

3. Wrap 1 pepper strip around 1 piece of cream cheese. Place on dough triangle. Fold over and pinch edges to seal; repeat with remaining pepper strips. Place 1 piece artichoke heart and 1 piece of cream cheese on dough triangle. Fold over and pinch edges to seal; repeat with remaining pieces of artichoke hearts. Wrap 1 strip salami around 1 piece of cream cheese. Place on dough triangle. Fold over and pinch edges to seal; repeat with remaining salami. Place 2 olive halves and 1 piece of cream cheese on dough triangle. Fold over and pinch edges to seal; repeat with remaining olives. Place evenly spaced on ungreased baking sheet. Brush with beaten egg.

4. Bake 12 to 14 minutes, or until golden brown. Cool on wire rack. Store in airtight container in refrigerator.

5. Reheat on baking sheet in preheated 325°F oven 7 to 8 minutes or until warmed through. Do not microwave.

Makes 16 pieces

Antipasto Crescent Bites

GLORIOUS GIFTS IN A JAR

HOT & SPICY MUSTARD

¼ cup whole yellow mustard seeds
¼ cup honey
3 tablespoons cider vinegar
2 tablespoons ground mustard
1 teaspoon salt
⅛ teaspoon ground cloves

1. Place ¼ cup water in small saucepan. Bring to a boil over high heat. Add mustard seeds. Cover saucepan; remove from heat. Let stand 1 hour or until liquid is absorbed.

2. Spoon mustard seeds into work bowl of food processor.

3. Add honey, vinegar, ground mustard, salt and cloves to work bowl; process using on/off pulsing action until mixture is thickened and seeds are coarsely chopped, scraping down side of work bowl once with spatula. Refrigerate at least 1 day before serving.

4. Store in airtight container in refrigerator up to 3 weeks.

Makes about 1 cup

Hot & Spicy Mustard

CRACKED PEPPERCORN HONEY MUSTARD

2½ cups Dijon mustard
1 jar (9.5 ounces) extra grainy Dijon mustard
¾ cup honey
2 tablespoons cracked black pepper
1 tablespoon dried tarragon leaves (optional)

1. Combine Dijon mustard, grainy Dijon mustard, honey, pepper and tarragon in medium bowl. Blend with wire whisk.

2. Spoon into 4 labeled 1¼-cup containers. Store refrigerated up to 4 weeks.   *Makes 4 (1¼-cup) containers*

ASIAN SPICY SWEET MUSTARD

1 jar (16 ounces) spicy brown mustard
1 cup peanut butter
¾ cup hoisin sauce
½ cup packed brown sugar

1. Combine mustard, peanut butter, hoisin sauce and sugar in medium bowl. Blend with wire whisk.

2. Spoon into 4 labeled 1-cup containers. Store refrigerated up to 4 weeks.   *Makes 4 (1-cup) containers*

HONEY THYME MUSTARD

1 cup Dijon mustard
½ cup honey
1 teaspoon crushed dried thyme leaves

Whisk together all ingredients in small bowl until well blended. Transfer mixture to airtight container and refrigerate until ready to use. Serve on sandwiches or brush over pork chops before broiling.   *Makes 1½ cups*

Favorite recipe from **National Honey Board**

Top to bottom: Asian Spicy Sweet Mustard and Cracked Peppercorn Honey Mustard

SPICY GERMAN MUSTARD

½ cup mustard seeds
2 tablespoons dry mustard
½ cup cold water
1 cup cider vinegar
1 small onion, chopped (about ¼ cup)
3 tablespoons packed brown sugar
2 cloves garlic, minced
¾ teaspoon salt
¼ teaspoon dried tarragon leaves
¼ teaspoon ground cinnamon

Combine mustard seeds, dry mustard and water in small bowl. Cover; let stand at least 4 hours or overnight.

Combine vinegar, onion, brown sugar, garlic, salt, tarragon and cinnamon in small saucepan. Bring to a boil over high heat; reduce heat to medium. Boil, uncovered, about 7 to 10 minutes until mixture is reduced by half.

Pour vinegar mixture through fine sieve into food processor bowl. Rinse saucepan; set aside. Add mustard mixture to vinegar mixture; process about 1 minute or until mustard seeds are chopped but not puréed. Pour into same saucepan. Cook over low heat until mustard is thick, stirring constantly. Store in airtight container or decorative gift jars up to 1 year in refrigerator. *Makes about 1 cup*

SWEET AND HOT MUSTARD SAUCE

½ cup (1.75 oz) dry mustard
½ teaspoon salt
¾ cup cider vinegar
¾ cup KARO® Light or Dark Corn Syrup
½ cup packed light brown sugar
1 teaspoon caraway seed, crushed (optional)
3 eggs

1. In medium saucepan combine mustard and salt. With wire whisk or fork, gradually stir in enough vinegar to make a smooth paste.

2. Stir in remaining vinegar, corn syrup, brown sugar and caraway seed. Add eggs one at a time, whisking until blended.

3. Stirring constantly, cook over medium heat until mixture thickens, about 10 minutes. Do not boil.

4. Spoon into 2 (½-pint) jars; cover. Refrigerate at least 24 hours before serving. *Makes about 2¼ cups*

RASPBERRY VINEGAR

1 bottle (12 ounces) white wine vinegar (1½ cups)
½ cup sugar
1 cup fresh raspberries or sliced strawberries, crushed

Combine vinegar and sugar in nonaluminum 2-quart saucepan. Heat until very hot, stirring occasionally. Do not boil. (If vinegar boils, it will become cloudy.)

Pour into glass bowl; stir in raspberries. Cover with plastic wrap. Let stand in cool place about 1 week until desired amount of flavor develops. Strain through fine mesh sieve or cheesecloth twice. Store up to 6 months in jar or bottle with tight-fitting lid in refrigerator.   *Makes about 2 cups vinegar*

HERBED VINEGAR

1½ cups white wine vinegar
½ cup fresh basil leaves

Pour vinegar into nonaluminum small saucepan. Heat until very hot, stirring occasionally. Do not boil. (If vinegar boils, it will become cloudy.)

Pour into glass bowl; add basil. Cover with plastic wrap. Let stand in cool place about 1 week until desired amount of flavor develops. Strain before using. Store up to 6 months in jar or bottle with tight-fitting lid.

Makes about 1½ cups vinegar

Variation: *Substitute 1 tablespoon of either fresh oregano, thyme, chervil or tarragon for the basil. Or, substitute cider vinegar for the wine vinegar.*

Italian Salad Dressing

ITALIAN SALAD DRESSING

½ cup extra virgin olive oil
¼ cup Basil-Garlic Champagne
    Vinegar (recipe follows)
1 teaspoon Dijon mustard
½ teaspoon salt
½ teaspoon sugar
¼ teaspoon ground black
    pepper

1. Whisk oil, Basil-Garlic Champagne Vinegar, mustard, salt, sugar and pepper in small bowl with wire whisk until well blended.

2. Place neck of funnel in decorative bottle. Line funnel with double layer of cheesecloth or coffee filter.

3. Pour mixture into funnel; discard solids. Seal bottle. Store in refrigerator up to 1 month. *Makes about ¾ cup*

BASIL-GARLIC CHAMPAGNE VINEGAR

¼ cup basil leaves
4 cloves garlic
4 dried hot red peppers
1¼ cups champagne sherry or aged sherry vinegar

1. Place basil leaves, garlic and peppers in jar.

2. Place sherry in small saucepan. Bring just to a boil over medium-high heat. (Bubbles will begin to form on the surface of the sherry.) Remove saucepan from heat.

3. Pour sherry into jar; cover.

4. Shake jar several times to distribute basil leaves. Store in cool dark place at least 7 days, shaking occasionally.

5. Place neck of funnel in decorative bottle. Line funnel with double layer of cheesecloth or coffee filter.

6. Pour vinegar mixture into funnel. Save peppers and basil and add to bottle, if desired; cover. Store in cool, dark place up to 2 months. *Makes 2 cups*

Make an Italian Theme gift basket for the pasta lover on your list. Start with a colander rather than a basket. Fill it with a bottle of Italian Salad Dressing, a jar of Sun-Dried Tomato Pesto (page 67), Savory Pull-Apart Loaves (page 110) and a package of imported pasta.

CITRUS-PLUM BARBECUE SAUCE

2 containers (12 ounces each) orange juice concentrate
2 jars (12 ounces each) plum preserves
½ cup honey
½ cup tomato paste
¼ cup dry sherry
2 tablespoons minced ginger
2 tablespoons soy sauce
2 cloves garlic, minced
½ teaspoon salt
½ teaspoon black pepper

1. Combine orange juice concentrate, plum preserves, honey, tomato paste, sherry, ginger, soy sauce, garlic, salt and pepper in large saucepan. Heat over medium-high heat until mixture begins to simmer. Reduce heat to medium-low; simmer 10 minutes. Cover and remove from heat. Cool 30 minutes.

2. Spoon into 4 labeled 12-ounce containers. Store refrigerated up to 3 weeks. *Makes 5½ to 6 cups*

HONEY BARBECUE BASTE

1 tablespoon vegetable oil
¼ cup minced onion
1 clove garlic, minced
1 can (8 ounces) tomato sauce
⅓ cup honey
3 tablespoons vinegar
2 tablespoons dry sherry
1 teaspoon dry mustard
½ teaspoon salt
¼ teaspoon coarsely ground black pepper

Heat oil in medium saucepan over medium heat until hot. Add onion and garlic; cook and stir until onion is tender. Add remaining ingredients. Bring to a boil; reduce heat to low and simmer 20 minutes. Serve over grilled chicken, pork, spareribs, salmon or hamburgers. *Makes 1 cup*

Favorite recipe from **National Honey Board**

Citrus-Plum Barbecue Sauce

Texas Hot & Tangy BBQ Sauce

¼ cup vegetable oil
2 cups finely chopped onion
6 cloves garlic, minced
2 cups water
1 can (12 ounces) tomato paste
1 cup packed brown sugar
¾ cup apple cider vinegar
½ cup molasses
¼ cup Worcestershire sauce
2 tablespoons jalapeño pepper sauce
2 teaspoons chili powder
2 teaspoons ground cumin
½ teaspoon ground red pepper

1. Heat oil in large skillet over medium-high heat 1 minute. Add onion; cook and stir 8 to 10 minutes or until onion begins to brown. Add garlic; cook 2 minutes longer or until onion is golden. Add water, tomato paste, sugar, vinegar, molasses, Worcestershire sauce, jalapeño pepper sauce, chili powder, cumin and ground red pepper. Stir with wire whisk until well blended. Reduce heat to medium-low; simmer 15 minutes, stirring occasionally. Cover and remove from heat. Cool 30 minutes.

2. Spoon into 4 labeled 12-ounce containers. Store refrigerated up to 3 weeks.   *Makes 5 to 5½ cups*

Smoky Honey Barbecue Sauce

1 cup honey
1 cup chili sauce
½ cup cider vinegar
1 teaspoon prepared mustard
1 teaspoon Worcestershire sauce
½ teaspoon pepper
½ teaspoon minced garlic
2 to 3 drops liquid smoke

Combine all ingredients except liquid smoke in medium saucepan over medium heat. Cook, stirring frequently, 20 to 30 minutes. Remove from heat; add liquid smoke to taste. Serve over grilled chicken, turkey, pork, spareribs, salmon or hamburgers.   *Makes about 2 cups*

Favorite recipe from **National Honey Board**

Texas Hot & Tangy BBQ Sauce

RIB TICKLIN' BARBECUE SAUCE

½ cup KARO® Light or Dark
    Corn Syrup
½ cup ketchup
½ cup finely chopped onion
¼ cup cider vinegar
¼ cup prepared mustard
¼ cup Worcestershire sauce

1. In 1½-quart saucepan combine corn syrup, ketchup, onion, vinegar, mustard and Worcestershire sauce. Stirring frequently, bring to boil over medium-high heat. Reduce heat; boil gently 15 minutes or until thickened.

2. Brush on chicken, ribs or beef during last 15 to 20 minutes of grilling, turning frequently. Heat remaining sauce to serve with meat. *Makes about 2 cups*

WYOMING WILD BARBECUE SAUCE

1 cup chili sauce
1 cup ketchup
¼ cup steak sauce
3 tablespoons dry mustard
2 tablespoons horseradish
2 tablespoons TABASCO®
    Pepper Sauce
1 tablespoon Worcestershire
    sauce
1 tablespoon garlic, finely
    chopped
1 tablespoon dark molasses
1 tablespoon red wine
    vinegar

Combine ingredients in medium bowl. Whisk until sauce is well blended. Store in 1-quart covered jar in refrigerator up to 7 days. Use as a baste while grilling beef, chicken, pork or game. *Makes 3 cups*

Clockwise from top left: Cranberry Chutney (page 92), Hot Red Pepper Jam (page 99) and Rib Ticklin' Barbecue Sauce

KOREAN-STYLE HONEY MARINADE

½ cup dry white wine
½ cup honey
½ cup soy sauce
2 green onions, chopped
2 tablespoons dark sesame
    oil
1 tablespoon grated fresh
    gingerroot
1 clove garlic, minced

Combine all ingredients in small bowl; mix thoroughly. Use to marinate steak or chicken.   *Makes about 1 ½ cups*

Favorite recipe from **National Honey Board**

GUAJILLO CHILE SAUCE

3 guajillo chiles*
1 pound fresh tomatillos,
    husks removed and
    washed
1 medium onion
1 clove garlic
½ teaspoon TABASCO® Pepper
    Sauce
½ teaspoon salt

These dried red chili peppers are about 4 inches long and extremely hot. They can sting and irritate the skin; wear rubber gloves when handling and do not touch your eyes. Wash your hands after handling.

Soften chiles on griddle over medium heat 1 minute. Remove stems and seeds. In 2½-quart saucepan, place chiles, tomatillos, onion and garlic; add water to barely cover. Heat to boiling; reduce heat and cook 15 minutes. Remove from heat and let stand 15 minutes longer. Drain and transfer ingredients to blender container. Add TABASCO® sauce and salt. Blend until smooth.   *Makes 2 cups*

Sun-Dried Tomato Pesto

1 tablespoon vegetable oil
½ cup pine nuts
2 cloves garlic
1 jar (8 ounces) sun-dried tomatoes packed in oil, undrained
1 cup Italian parsley
½ cup grated Parmesan cheese
¼ cup coarsely chopped pitted Kalamata olives
2 teaspoons dried basil leaves
¼ teaspoon crushed red pepper

1. Heat oil in small skillet over medium-low heat. Add pine nuts; cook 30 to 45 seconds or until lightly browned, shaking pan constantly.

2. Remove nuts from skillet with slotted spoon; drain on paper towels.

3. Combine pine nuts and garlic in work bowl of food processor. Process using on/off pulsing action until mixture is finely chopped.

4. Add undrained tomatoes to work bowl; process until finely chopped. Add parsley, cheese, olives, basil and pepper; process until mixture resembles thick paste, scraping down side of bowl occasionally with small spatula.

5. Spoon pesto into decorative crock or jar with tight-fitting lid; cover.

6. Store in airtight container in refrigerator up to 1 month.

Makes about 1½ cups

Left to right: Refrigerator Corn Relish and Quick Refrigerator Sweet Pickles (page 70)

REFRIGERATOR CORN RELISH

**2 cups cut fresh corn (4 ears)
or 1 (10-ounce) package
frozen whole-kernel corn**
½ cup vinegar
⅓ cup cold water
1 tablespoon cornstarch
¼ cup chopped onion
¼ cup chopped celery
**¼ cup chopped green or red
bell pepper**
**2 tablespoons chopped
pimiento**
1 teaspoon ground turmeric
½ teaspoon salt
½ teaspoon dry mustard
**1¾ teaspoons EQUAL®
MEASURE™ or 6 packets
EQUAL® sweetener or
¼ cup EQUAL®
SPOONFUL™**

Cook corn in boiling water until crisp-tender, 5 to 7 minutes; drain and set aside. Combine vinegar, water and cornstarch in large saucepan; stir until cornstarch is dissolved. Add corn, onion, celery, pepper, pimiento, turmeric, salt and mustard. Cook and stir until thickened and bubbly. Cook and stir 2 minutes more. Remove from heat; stir in Equal®. Cool. Cover and store in refrigerator up to 2 weeks. Serve with beef, pork or poultry. *Makes 2½ cups*

ZUCCHINI CHOW CHOW

2 cups thinly sliced zucchini
2 cups thinly sliced yellow
    summer squash
½ cup thinly sliced red onion
    Salt
1½ cups cider vinegar
1 to 1¼ cups sugar
1½ tablespoons pickling spice
1 cup thinly sliced carrots
1 small red bell pepper, thinly
    sliced

1. Sprinkle zucchini, summer squash and onion lightly with salt; let stand in colander 30 minutes. Rinse well with cold water; drain thoroughly. Pat dry with paper towels.

2. Combine vinegar, sugar and pickling spice in medium saucepan. Bring to a boil over high heat. Add carrots and bell pepper; bring to a boil. Remove from heat; cool to room temperature.

3. Spoon zucchini, summer squash, onion and carrot mixture into sterilized jars; cover and refrigerate up to 3 weeks.

Makes about 8 cups

QUICK REFRIGERATOR SWEET PICKLES

5 cups thinly sliced cucumbers
2 cloves garlic, halved
2 cups water
1 teaspoon mustard seed
1 teaspoon celery seed
1 teaspoon ground turmeric
2 cups sliced onions
1 cup julienne carrot strips
2 cups vinegar
3 tablespoons plus
    1¾ teaspoons EQUAL®
    MEASURE™ or
    36 packets EQUAL®
    sweetener or 1½ cups
    EQUAL® SPOONFUL™

Place cucumbers and garlic in glass bowl. Combine water, mustard seed, celery seed and turmeric in medium saucepan. Bring to boiling. Add onion and carrots; cook 2 minutes. Add vinegar; bring just to boiling. Remove from heat; stir in Equal®. Pour over cucumbers and garlic. Cool. Cover and chill at least 24 hours before serving. Store in refrigerator up to 2 weeks.

Makes about 6 cups

Zucchini Chow Chow

PINEAPPLE-PEACH SALSA

2 cans (20 ounces each)
pineapple tidbits in juice,
drained
2 cans (15 ounces each)
peach slices in juice,
drained and chopped
1 can (15 ounces) black
beans, rinsed and
drained
¼ cup finely chopped red bell
pepper
2 jalapeño peppers,* seeded
and chopped
2 tablespoons chopped fresh
cilantro
2 tablespoons lime juice
2 tablespoons red wine
vinegar
½ teaspoon salt
¼ teaspoon ground red pepper
¼ teaspoon garlic powder

*Jalapeño peppers can sting and
irritate the skin; wear rubber
gloves when handling peppers
and do not touch eyes.

1. Combine pineapple, peaches, beans, red bell pepper,
jalapeño peppers, cilantro, lime juice, vinegar, salt, ground
red pepper and garlic powder in large bowl; toss to coat.

2. Spoon into 4 labeled 1¾-cup containers. Store in
containers in refrigerator up to 2 weeks.

Makes 4 (1¾-cup) containers

Pineapple-Peach Salsa

ROASTED PEPPER & TOMATO SALSA

3 yellow or red bell peppers
2 poblano peppers
1 large onion
4 cloves garlic, minced
2 tablespoons olive oil
1 teaspoon dried oregano
¾ teaspoon salt
½ teaspoon black pepper
2 cans diced tomatoes
¾ cup tomato juice
¼ cup chopped fresh cilantro
1 tablespoon lime juice

1. Preheat oven to 350°F. Chop peppers and onion into ¾-inch pieces. Combine peppers, onion, garlic, olive oil, oregano, salt and black pepper in large bowl; toss to coat. Spread onto two 15×10×1-inch baking pans. Bake 20 minutes or until peppers and onion are lightly browned, stirring after 10 minutes.

2. Combine roasted vegetables and remaining ingredients in large bowl. Spoon into 4 labeled 1½-cup storage containers. Store in refrigerator up to 10 days or freeze up to 2 months.

Makes 4 (1½-cup) containers

CRANBERRY SALSA

2 cups fresh or frozen whole cranberries
1 orange, peeled and chopped
1 tablespoon grated orange peel
1 tablespoon minced fresh gingerroot
1 tablespoon chopped fresh parsley
1 tablespoon chopped fresh cilantro
1 jalapeño pepper, seeded and chopped
⅓ cup honey
2 tablespoons thawed frozen orange juice concentrate

Coarsely chop cranberries in food processor. Add orange, orange peel, ginger, parsley, cilantro and jalapeño pepper; process 30 to 40 seconds or until mixture is coarsely chopped. Add honey and orange juice concentrate; process about 5 seconds more. Serve with turkey or other poultry.

Makes 2 cups

Favorite recipe from **National Honey Board**

Roasted Pepper & Tomato Salsa

RIO GRANDE SALSA

1 tablespoon vegetable oil
1 onion, chopped
3 cloves garlic, minced
2 teaspoons ground cumin
1½ teaspoons chili powder
2 cans (14½ ounces each)
    diced tomatoes, drained
1 canned chipotle chili pepper,
    in adobo sauce, seeded
    and finely diced*
1 teaspoon adobo sauce from
    canned chili
½ cup chopped fresh cilantro
    leaves
¾ teaspoon sugar
½ teaspoon salt

*Chipotle chili peppers are smoked jalapeño peppers and are commonly available canned in adobo sauce. Chipotle chili peppers can sting and irritate the skin; wear rubber gloves when handling peppers and do not touch eyes. Wash hands after handling chili peppers.

1. Heat oil in medium saucepan over medium-high heat until hot. Add onion and garlic. Cook and stir 5 minutes or until onion is tender. Add cumin and chili powder; cook 30 seconds, stirring frequently. Add tomatoes, chipotle chili and adobo sauce. Reduce heat to medium-low. Simmer 10 to 12 minutes or until salsa is thickened, stirring occasionally.

2. Remove saucepan from heat; stir in cilantro, sugar and salt. Cool completely. Store in airtight container in refrigerator up to 3 weeks. *Makes about 3 cups*

Rio Grande Salsa

FRESH MELON SALSA

3 cups diced melon
6 tablespoons lime juice
¼ cup honey
¼ cup diced red bell pepper
1½ tablespoons finely chopped cilantro
1 tablespoon seeded, minced jalapeño pepper
½ teaspoon salt

Combine all ingredients in large bowl; mix well. Refrigerate overnight to allow flavors to blend. Serve over grilled fish or chicken. *Makes 3 cups*

Favorite recipe from **National Honey Board**

HOLIDAY APPLE CHUTNEY

9 (½-pint) jelly jars with lids and screw bands
8 large tart apples, peeled, cored and chopped (about 4 pounds)
2 large onions, chopped
2 cups golden raisins
1 package (16 ounces) packed brown sugar (2¼ cups)
2 cups granulated sugar
1 cup cider vinegar
Grated peel and juice of 2 oranges and 1 lemon
2 tablespoons finely chopped crystallized ginger
2 teaspoons ground cinnamon
½ teaspoon ground cloves

Wash jars, lids and bands. Leave jars in hot water. Place lids and bands in large pan of water.

Combine remaining ingredients in heavy 8-quart saucepan or Dutch oven. Bring to a boil over high heat. Reduce heat to medium-low. Simmer, uncovered, 30 minutes or until mixture thickens, stirring frequently.

Bring water with lids and bands to a boil. Ladle hot mixture into hot jars leaving ½-inch space at top. Run metal spatula around inside of jar to remove air bubbles. Wipe tops and sides of jar rims clean. Place hot lids and bands on jar. Screw bands tightly, but do not force. To process, place jars in boiling water; boil 10 minutes. Remove jars with tongs; cool on wire racks. (Check seals by pressing on lid with fingertip; lid should remain concave.) Label and date jars. Store unopened jars in a cool, dry place up to 12 months. Refrigerate after opening up to 6 months.
Makes 9 (½-pint) jars

TOMATO CHUTNEY

4 cups peeled, seeded and
    diced tomatoes
3 medium apples, peeled,
    cored and diced
2 cups coarsely chopped
    onions
1 cup diced red pepper
⅔ cup packed brown sugar
½ cup raisins
2 cloves garlic, minced
1 teaspoon salt
1 teaspoon ground ginger
½ teaspoon cinnamon
¼ teaspoon ground allspice
¼ teaspoon ground red pepper
1 cup KARO® Light or Dark
    Corn Syrup
⅔ cup cider vinegar

1. In large saucepan combine tomatoes, apples, onions, red pepper, brown sugar, raisins, garlic, salt, ginger, cinnamon, allspice and ground red pepper.

2. Bring to boil over medium-high heat. Reduce heat; simmer partially covered until onion is translucent, about 20 minutes.

3. Add corn syrup and vinegar. Cook uncovered over medium heat, stirring frequently, until mixture thickens, about 30 minutes. If desired, ladle into jars. Cover; refrigerate.

Makes 5½ cups

Top to bottom: Carrot-Walnut Chutney (page 82) and Chunky Fruit Chutney

CHUNKY FRUIT CHUTNEY

**2 cans (15¼ ounces each)
tropical fruit salad
packed in light syrup and
passion fruit juice**

**1 can (15 ounces) apricot
halves in extra light
syrup**

**1 cup chopped green bell
pepper**

1 cup chopped red bell pepper

¼ cup packed brown sugar

1 teaspoon curry powder

1 teaspoon onion powder

½ teaspoon salt

½ teaspoon garlic powder

½ teaspoon ground ginger

½ teaspoon red pepper flakes

**½ teaspoon coarse ground
black pepper**

1. Drain tropical fruit salad, reserving ½ cup liquid. Drain apricots; discard syrup. Chop fruit salad and apricots into ½-inch pieces.

2. Combine bell peppers, reserved ½ cup juice, sugar, curry powder, onion powder, salt, garlic powder, ginger, red pepper flakes and black pepper in large skillet. Bring to a boil over high heat. Reduce heat to medium-high; simmer 6 to 8 minutes or until most liquid is evaporated and bell peppers are tender. Remove from heat. Stir in chopped fruit.

3. Spoon into 4 labeled 1¼-cup containers. Store in refrigerator up to 4 weeks.   *Makes 4 (1¼-cup) containers*

This tropical chutney, bursting with fresh flavor, is the perfect accompaniment to chicken, fish or pork.

CRANBERRY-APPLE RELISH

1 package (12 ounces) fresh or frozen cranberries
1 apple, peeled and cut into eighths
½ cup packed fresh mint leaves
⅓ cup golden or dark raisins
⅓ cup packed brown sugar
⅓ cup orange marmalade
1 tablespoon lemon juice
1 tablespoon Dijon mustard

1. Combine cranberries, apple and mint in food processor; process until finely chopped.

2. Transfer cranberry mixture to medium bowl. Add raisins, brown sugar, marmalade, lemon juice and mustard; mix well. Spoon into 4 labeled 1-cup containers. Store in refrigerator up to 2 weeks. Serve with roasted poultry, pork or lamb.

Makes 4 (1-cup) containers

CARROT-WALNUT CHUTNEY

1 pound fresh carrots, peeled and chopped into ½-inch pieces
2 tablespoons vegetable oil
1½ cups chopped onions
¾ cup packed brown sugar
¼ cup apple cider vinegar
1 teaspoon ground allspice
1 teaspoon ground cumin
½ teaspoon black pepper
½ teaspoon ground cinnamon
¼ teaspoon salt
1 cup raisins
1½ cups chopped toasted walnuts

1. Place carrots and ⅓ cup water in large saucepan; cover. Bring to a boil over high heat; reduce heat to low. Simmer 8 to 10 minutes or until tender; drain.

2. Heat oil in large skillet over medium-high heat 1 minute. Add onions; cook and stir 6 to 8 minutes or until golden brown. Stir in sugar, vinegar, allspice, cumin, pepper, cinnamon and salt; simmer 1 minute. Add raisins; simmer 3 minutes. Remove from heat; stir in carrots and walnuts. Spoon into 4 labeled 1-cup containers. Store in refrigerator up to 4 weeks.

Makes 4 (1-cup) containers

Cranberry-Apple Relish

GINGERED APPLE-CRANBERRY CHUTNEY

2 medium Granny Smith apples, peeled and chopped
1 package (12 ounces) fresh or thawed frozen cranberries
1¼ cups packed light brown sugar
¾ cup cranberry juice cocktail
½ cup golden raisins
¼ cup chopped crystallized ginger
¼ cup cider vinegar
1 teaspoon ground cinnamon
⅛ teaspoon ground allspice

1. Combine apples, cranberries, sugar, cranberry juice cocktail, raisins, ginger, vinegar, cinnamon and allspice in medium saucepan.

2. Bring to a boil over high heat. Reduce heat to medium. Simmer 20 minutes or until mixture is very thick, stirring occasionally.

3. Remove saucepan from heat. Cool completely. Store in airtight container in refrigerator up to 2 weeks.

Makes about 3 cups

HONEY RHUBARB COMPOTE

⅔ cup honey
1 cup water
4 cups coarsely chopped rhubarb (½-inch pieces)
½ teaspoon vanilla
2 tablespoons cornstarch
3 tablespoons cold water

Dissolve honey in water in large nonaluminum saucepan. Bring to a boil over medium-high heat. Add rhubarb. Reduce heat to low; simmer, uncovered, 15 to 25 minutes or until rhubarb is tender but still intact. Stir in vanilla. Combine cornstarch with 3 tablespoons water; mix well. Gradually stir cornstarch mixture into rhubarb; cook and stir until mixture comes to a boil. Reduce heat; simmer 3 to 5 minutes or until mixture thickens. Pour into serving bowl and refrigerate until cold.

Makes 6 servings

Favorite recipe from **National Honey Board**

Gingered Apple-Cranberry Chutney

GAZPACHO RELISH

4 teaspoons tomato paste
2 teaspoons red wine vinegar
2 teaspoons lime juice
1½ teaspoons olive oil
½ pound tomatoes, peeled,
    seeded and chopped
¼ cup minced green bell
    pepper
¼ cup peeled and chopped
    cucumber
4 canned artichoke hearts,
    chopped
2 teaspoons minced shallots
2 teaspoons chopped fresh
    dill
¼ teaspoon black pepper
3 to 6 drops hot pepper sauce

Place tomato paste, vinegar, juice and oil in blender or food processor; process until smooth. Transfer mixture to medium bowl and stir in remaining ingredients. Cover and refrigerate several hours before serving. Serve cold. Refrigerate leftovers.

Makes 1 cup

Favorite recipe from **Bob Evans**®

SWEET & SOUR RELISH

1 medium onion, chopped
1 stalk celery, chopped
½ cup prepared chili sauce
2 tablespoons dark brown
    sugar
2 tablespoons cider vinegar
    Dash dried tarragon leaves

Combine ingredients in medium saucepan. Bring to a boil over medium-high heat. Reduce heat to low; simmer 5 minutes, stirring occasionally. Serve hot or cold.

Makes 1 cup

Favorite recipe from **Bob Evans**®

Top to bottom: Sweet & Sour Relish and Gazpacho Relish

CHOCOLATE-CHERRY CHUTNEY

2 jars (16 ounces each)
   maraschino cherries
8 ounces semisweet
   chocolate, coarsely
   chopped
1 can (5 ounces) evaporated
   milk
1 cup powdered sugar
1½ cups slivered or chopped
   toasted almonds
1 cup white chocolate chips

1. Drain cherries, reserving ¼ cup juice. Coarsely chop cherries; set aside.

2. Melt semisweet chocolate and evaporated milk in microwave on HIGH 3 to 4 minutes or until melted, stirring after 2 minutes. Add powdered sugar and reserved juice. Microwave 1 minute; stir until smooth. Stir in chopped cherries, toasted almonds and white chocolate chips.

3. Spoon into 4 labeled 1¼-cup containers. Store refrigerated up to 4 weeks.　　*Makes 4 (1¼-cup) containers*

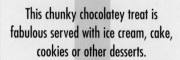

This chunky chocolatey treat is
fabulous served with ice cream, cake,
cookies or other desserts.

Chocolate-Cherry Chutney

EGGPLANT CHUTNEY

2 large eggplants
    (2½ pounds), unpeeled
    and cut into ½-inch
    cubes
1 small onion, finely chopped
3 tablespoons minced garlic
3 tablespoons minced fresh
    ginger
3 tablespoons packed light
    brown sugar
1 teaspoon dried rosemary
    leaves
1 teaspoon dried anise or
    fennel seeds
½ teaspoon dried thyme
    leaves
2 tablespoons balsamic
    vinegar
1 tablespoon dark sesame oil
¼ cup dark raisins
½ cup reduced-sodium chicken
    broth
2 tablespoons coarsely
    chopped walnuts

1. Preheat oven to 450°F. Arrange eggplant on 15×10-inch jelly-roll pan lined with foil. Add onion, garlic, ginger, brown sugar, rosemary, anise and thyme; toss to combine. Drizzle with vinegar and oil; stir to coat. Bake 1½ hours or until eggplant is browned and shriveled, stirring every 30 minutes.

2. Stir raisins into eggplant mixture and drizzle with chicken broth; bake 10 minutes or until broth is absorbed. Remove from oven; stir in walnuts. Cool. Serve on crackers or lavash as an appetizer, or serve warm or at room temperature as a condiment with roasted meats and poultry, if desired. Store chutney in airtight container up to 10 days in refrigerator or 3 months in freezer. *Makes about 2¾ cups*

Eggplant Chutney

CRANBERRY CHUTNEY

2 bags (12 ounces each) cranberries
2 cups sugar
1 cup chopped onions
1 cup golden raisins
3 cloves garlic, minced
1 tablespoon minced fresh ginger
1½ teaspoons salt
1 teaspoon ground allspice
¼ teaspoon cinnamon
¼ teaspoon ground cloves
1 cup KARO® Light or Dark Corn Syrup
1 cup cider vinegar
1 cup chopped walnuts

1. In large saucepan combine cranberries, sugar, onions, raisins, garlic, ginger, salt, allspice, cinnamon and cloves. Bring to boil over medium-high heat. Reduce heat.

2. Stirring occasionally, simmer partially covered until onions are translucent, about 15 minutes.

3. Add corn syrup, vinegar and walnuts. Stirring frequently, cook uncovered over medium heat until mixture thickens, about 15 minutes.

4. Ladle into jars. Store in refrigerator.   *Makes 6 cups*

SPICED FRUIT BUTTER

3 pounds apples, pears or peaches
¾ cup apple juice, pear nectar or peach nectar
1 to 2 teaspoons ground cinnamon
½ teaspoon ground nutmeg
⅛ teaspoon ground cloves
5 teaspoons EQUAL® MEASURE™ or 16 packets EQUAL® sweetener or ⅔ cup EQUAL® SPOONFUL™

• Peel and core or pit fruit; slice. Combine prepared fruit, fruit juice and spices in Dutch oven. Bring to boiling; cover and simmer until very tender, about 15 minutes. Cool slightly. Purée in batches in blender or food processor. Return to Dutch oven.

• Simmer, uncovered, over low heat until desired consistency, stirring frequently. (This may take up to 1 hour.) Remove from heat; stir in Equal®. Transfer to freezer containers or jars, leaving ½-inch headspace. Store up to 2 weeks in refrigerator or up to 3 months in freezer.

Makes 6 (½-pint) jars

CHRISTMAS CITRUS MARMALADE

2 lemons
1 orange
2½ cups water
⅛ teaspoon baking soda
1 large grapefruit
7 (½-pint) jelly jars with lids and screw bands
1 box (1¾ ounces) powdered fruit pectin
6 cups sugar

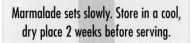

Marmalade sets slowly. Store in a cool, dry place 2 weeks before serving.

Remove peel of lemons and orange in long strips, making sure there is no white on the peel. Stack strips; cut into thin slivers. Combine lemon and orange peels, water and baking soda in 2-quart saucepan. Bring to a boil over high heat. Reduce heat to low; cover and simmer 20 minutes, stirring occasionally.

Meanwhile, peel grapefruit. Remove white pith from grapefruit, lemons and orange; discard peel and pith. Separate fruit into sections. With fingers, remove pulp from membrane of each section over large saucepan to save juice. Dice fruit sections into same saucepan. Bring to a boil. Cover and simmer 10 minutes. Measure 5 cups fruit mixture into 6-quart saucepan or Dutch oven.

Wash jars, lids and bands. Leave jars in hot water. Place lids and bands in large pan of water. Mix pectin into fruit mixture. Bring to a rolling boil over medium-high heat, stirring constantly. Immediately stir in sugar. Bring to a rolling boil and boil 1 minute, stirring constantly. Remove from heat; skim off foam with metal spoon.

Bring water with lids and bands to a boil. Ladle hot mixture into hot jars leaving ½-inch space at top. Run metal spatula around inside of jar to remove air bubbles. Wipe tops and sides of jar rims clean. Place hot lids and bands on jar. Screw bands tightly, but do not force. To process, place jars in boiling water; boil 10 minutes. Remove jars with tongs; cool on wire racks. (Check seals by pressing on lid with fingertip; lid should remain concave.) Store unopened jars in a cool, dry place up to 12 months. Refrigerate after opening up to 6 months. *Makes about seven ½-pint jars*

Homestyle Mixed Berry Freezer Jam

HOMESTYLE MIXED BERRY FREEZER JAM

1 package (16 ounces) frozen mixed berries, thawed
3¾ cups sugar
2 teaspoons grated orange peel (optional)
1 pouch (3 ounces) liquid pectin
2 tablespoons orange juice

1. Place berries in food processor or blender; process until pieces are about ¼ inch in size. Combine berries, sugar and orange peel in large bowl; stir 2 minutes. Let stand 10 minutes.

2. Combine pectin and orange juice in small bowl; stir into berry mixture. Stir 2 minutes to blend thoroughly. Spoon into 4 labeled 1-cup freezer containers, leaving ½-inch space at top of container. Cover with tight-fitting lids. Let stand 24 hours to set. Refrigerate up to 3 weeks or freeze up to 6 months.

Makes 4 (1-cup) containers

CRANBERRY-PEACH FREEZER JAM

3 cups (12 ounces) fresh or frozen cranberries, thawed
2 cups coarsely chopped fresh peaches
6 cups sugar
¾ cup peach nectar
1 teaspoon grated fresh ginger (optional)
2 pouches (3 ounces each) liquid pectin
¼ cup lemon juice

1. Place cranberries in food processor or blender; process until pieces are ⅛ inch in size. Transfer to large bowl. Place peaches in food processor or blender; process until pieces are ¼ inch in size. Add peaches, sugar, peach nectar and ginger to cranberries; stir 2 minutes. Let stand 10 minutes.

2. Combine pectin and lemon juice in small bowl; stir into fruit mixture. Stir 2 minutes to mix thoroughly.

3. Spoon into 7 labeled 1-cup freezer containers, leaving ½-inch space at top. Cover with tight-fitting lids. Let stand 24 hours to set. Refrigerate up to 3 weeks or freeze up to 6 months.

Makes 7 (1-cup) containers

Honey Strawberry Preserves

6 cups sliced strawberries
2 boxes (1¾ ounces each) powdered pectin
1¾ cups honey
2 tablespoons lemon juice

Combine strawberries and pectin in large saucepan; crush berries to blend completely. Bring mixture to a full rolling boil over medium-high heat. Boil hard 1 minute, stirring constantly. Stir in honey and lemon juice; return to a full rolling boil. Boil hard 5 minutes, stirring constantly. Remove from heat. Skim off foam. Ladle into clean, hot canning jars to within ¼ inch of tops. Seal according to manufacturer's directions. Place jars on rack in canner. Process 10 minutes in boiling water bath with boiling water 2 inches above jar tops. Remove jars from canner. Place on thick cloth or wire rack; cool away from drafts. After 12 hours test lids for proper seal; remove rings from sealed jars.   *Makes 3 pints*

Favorite recipe from **National Honey Board**

Peach Preserves

2½ to 3 pounds ripe peaches (10 to 12)
2 tablespoons lemon juice
1 package (1¾ ounces) no-sugar-needed pectin
7¼ teaspoons EQUAL® MEASURE™ or 24 packets EQUAL® sweetener or 1 cup EQUAL® SPOONFUL™

• Peel, pit and finely chop peaches; measure 4 cups into saucepan. Stir in lemon juice and pectin. Let stand 10 minutes, stirring frequently. Cook and stir until boiling. Cook and stir 1 minute more. Remove from heat; stir in Equal®. Skim off foam.

• Immediately ladle into freezer containers or jars, leaving ½-inch headspace. Seal and label containers. Let stand at room temperature several hours or until set. Store up to 2 weeks in refrigerator or 6 months in freezer.   *Makes 8 (½-pint) jars*

Clockwise from top: Honey Citrus Syrup (page 100), Honey Chocolate Sauce (page 101) and Honey Strawberry Preserves

CHAMPAGNE-STRAWBERRY FREEZER JAM

4 cups fresh strawberries (about 2 pints)
1½ cups champagne
3 cups sugar
1 box (1.75 ounces) fruit pectin for lower sugar recipes

1. Place strawberries in food processor or blender; process until pieces are about ¼ inch in size. Measure 3¼ cups; set aside.

2. Bring champagne to a boil over high heat in medium saucepan. Reduce heat to medium-low; simmer 5 minutes. Remove from heat; let stand 15 minutes. Return champagne to 2-cup measuring cup; add enough water to equal 1 cup.

3. Combine sugar and pectin in medium bowl; blend well. Combine sugar mixture and champagne in large saucepan. Bring to a boil over medium-high heat, stirring constantly. Continue boiling 1 minute longer, stirring constantly. Remove from heat. Add strawberries; stir 1 minute.

4. Spoon into 5 labeled 1-cup freezer containers, leaving ½-inch space at top of container. Cover with tight-fitting lids. Let stand at room temperature 24 hours to set. Refrigerate up to 3 weeks or freeze up to 6 months.

Makes 5 (1-cup) containers

CHUNKY APPLESAUCE

10 tart apples (about 3 pounds) peeled, cored and chopped
¾ cup packed light brown sugar
½ cup apple juice or apple cider
1½ teaspoons ground cinnamon
⅛ teaspoon salt
⅛ teaspoon ground nutmeg

1. Combine apples, brown sugar, apple juice, cinnamon, salt and nutmeg in heavy, large saucepan; cover. Cook over medium-low heat 40 to 45 minutes or until apples are tender, stirring occasionally with wooden spoon to break apples into chunks. Remove saucepan from heat. Cool completely.

2. Store in airtight container in refrigerator up to 1 month.

Makes about 5½ cups

HOT RED PEPPER JAM

**3 small red bell peppers
(about 1 lb)**
3 jalapeño peppers
3 cups sugar
**1 cup KARO® Light Corn
Syrup**
¾ cup cider vinegar
¼ teaspoon salt
**1 pouch (3 ounces) liquid fruit
pectin**

1. Wash, seed and cut peppers into 1-inch pieces. In blender or food processor, finely chop peppers; measure 1½ cups.

2. In 8-quart stainless steel or enamel saucepot, combine peppers, sugar, corn syrup, vinegar and salt. Stirring frequently, bring to full rolling boil over high heat. Stirring constantly, boil 5 minutes. Remove from heat.

3. Stir in pectin until well blended. With metal spoon, skim off foam.

4. Ladle into clean hot ½-pint jars, leaving ¼-inch headspace. Wipe top edge with damp cloth. Seal according to jar manufacturer's directions.

5. Process in boiling-water bath 10 minutes.

6. Cool on wire rack or folded towel. To prevent floating peppers, turn jars upside down after 15 minutes of cooling, then turn right side up and allow to finish cooling.

Makes about 5 (½-pint) jars

Green Pepper Jam: *Follow recipe for Hot Red Pepper Jam. Omit red bell peppers. Use 3 large green bell peppers. If desired, add 2 to 3 drops green food color with fruit pectin.*

Yellow Pepper Jam: *Follow recipe for Hot Red Pepper Jam. Omit red bell peppers. Use 3 large yellow bell peppers. If desired, add 2 to 3 drops yellow food color with fruit pectin.*

HONEY CITRUS SYRUP

½ cup honey
¼ cup lemon juice
¼ cup orange juice

Combine all ingredients in small bowl; stir until well blended. Refrigerate in airtight container until ready to use. Use syrup to sweeten tea and glaze fruits. *Makes 1 cup*

Favorite recipe from **National Honey Board**

GOOEY HOT FUDGE SAUCE

2 cups (12 ounces) semisweet chocolate chips
2 tablespoons butter
½ cup half-and-half
1 tablespoon corn syrup
⅛ teaspoon salt
½ teaspoon vanilla extract

Melt chocolate and butter with half-and-half, corn syrup and salt in medium saucepan over low heat, stirring until smooth. Remove from heat; let stand 10 minutes. Stir in vanilla. Serve warm or pour into clean glass jars and seal tightly. Store up to 6 months in refrigerator. Reheat sauce in double-boiler over hot (not boiling) water before serving, if desired.

Makes about 1½ cups sauce

CREAMY CARAMEL SAUCE

1 cup granulated sugar
1 cup whipping cream
½ cup packed light brown sugar
⅓ cup corn syrup
1 teaspoon vanilla extract

Place granulated sugar, cream, brown sugar and corn syrup in medium saucepan. Stir over low heat until mixture boils. Carefully clip candy thermometer to side of pan. (Do not let bulb touch bottom of pan.) Cook, stirring occasionally, about 20 minutes or until thermometer registers 238°F. Immediately remove from heat. Stir in vanilla. Cool about 15 minutes. Serve warm or pour into clean glass jars and seal tightly. Store up to 6 months in refrigerator. Reheat sauce over low heat before serving. *Makes about 2 cups sauce*

Butterscotch Sauce

¾ cup packed light brown sugar
½ cup KARO® Light or Dark Corn Syrup
2 tablespoons MAZOLA® Margarine or butter
½ cup heavy or whipping cream
1 teaspoon vanilla

1. In 1-quart saucepan combine brown sugar, corn syrup and margarine.

2. Stirring frequently, bring to full boil over medium heat and boil 1 minute. Remove from heat; immediately stir in cream and vanilla.

3. Cool; serve over ice-cream or desserts.

4. Store in refrigerator. Stir before serving.

Makes about 1½ cups

Peanut Butter Fudge Sauce

½ cup KARO® Light or Dark Corn Syrup
½ cup SKIPPY® Creamy Peanut Butter
¼ cup heavy or whipping cream
½ cup semisweet chocolate chips

In 1½-quart microwavable bowl combine corn syrup, peanut butter and cream. Microwave on HIGH 1½ minutes or until boiling. Add chocolate chips; stir until melted. Serve warm over ice cream. Store in refrigerator.

Makes about 1¼ cups

Note: *To reheat, microwave uncovered on LOW (30%) about 1½ minutes, just until pourable.*

Honey Chocolate Sauce

1½ cups honey
1½ cups unsweetened cocoa
2 tablespoons butter or margarine

Combine all ingredients; mix well. Cover with waxed paper and microwave at HIGH (100% power) 2 to 2½ minutes, stirring after 1 minute. Pour into sterilized gift jars. Keep refrigerated.

Makes 2½ cups

Favorite recipe from **National Honey Board**

102

Spiced Peach Sauce

SPICED PEACH SAUCE

2 pounds frozen sliced
   unsweetened peaches,
   thawed
2 cups sugar
1½ teaspoons lemon juice
1½ teaspoons ground cinnamon
¼ teaspoon ground nutmeg

1. Combine peaches and thawing liquid, sugar, lemon juice, cinnamon and nutmeg in medium saucepan.

2. Bring to a boil over high heat. Boil 45 to 50 minutes or until thickened, stirring occasionally and breaking peaches into small pieces with back of wooden spoon. Remove saucepan from heat; cool completely.

3. Store in airtight container in refrigerator up to 2 months.

Makes about 3 cups

ALMOND-CRANBERRY SYRUP

1 package (12 ounces) frozen
   cranberries, thawed
1 cup sugar
¾ cup corn syrup
¼ teaspoon almond extract
   (optional)

1. Combine cranberries and ¼ cup water in medium saucepan. Bring to a boil over high heat. Boil 10 minutes or until cranberries are tender and pop, stirring frequently.

2. Add sugar and corn syrup to saucepan. Bring to a boil over high heat. Boil 10 minutes or until mixture thickens and coats spoon, stirring constantly. Remove saucepan from heat.

3. Place wire mesh sieve over medium bowl. Pour cranberry mixture into sieve, pressing cranberries with back of wooden spoon to extract all of juices. Add almond extract. Cool completely. Reserve cranberries for another use.*

4. When syrup has cooled completely, strain again in wire mesh sieve; discard solids.

5. To transfer syrup to decorative glass bottle, place neck of funnel in bottle. Pour syrup into funnel. Remove funnel; seal bottle. Store in airtight container in refrigerator up to 2 months.

Makes about 1¾ cups

Spoon cranberries into decorative jar; cover. Serve as a spread.

RICH CHOCOLATE SAUCE

1 cup whipping cream
⅓ cup light corn syrup
1 cup (6 ounces) semisweet
     chocolate chips
1 to 2 tablespoons dark rum
     (optional)
1 teaspoon vanilla

Place cream and corn syrup in small saucepan. Stir over medium heat until mixture boils. Remove from heat. Stir in chocolate, rum, if desired, and vanilla until chocolate is melted. Cool 10 minutes. Serve warm or pour into clean glass jars and seal tightly. Store up to 6 months in refrigerator. Reheat sauce over low heat before serving.

Makes about 1¾ cups sauce

MOCHA ESPRESSO MIX

4 ounces semisweet chocolate
     (squares or bars), grated
¾ cup nonfat dry milk powder
½ cup espresso powder
½ teaspoon ground cinnamon

Combine all ingredients in small bowl until well blended. Spoon mixture into decorative glass jar with tight-fitting lid; cover. Store at room temperature up to 1 month.

Makes about 1⅔ cups

For single serving: Place 2 rounded tablespoons Mocha Espresso Mix in mug or cup; add ¾ cup boiling water. Stir until mix is dissolved. Serve with whipped cream, if desired.

CROCK OF SPICE FOR APPLE CIDER

**12 cinnamon sticks, broken
into small pieces**
¼ cup whole cloves
¼ cup allspice berries
¼ cup juniper berries
**1 tablespoon dried orange
peel, chopped**
**1 tablespoon dried lemon
peel, chopped**
1 teaspoon ground nutmeg

Combine all ingredients in small bowl until well blended. Spoon into airtight container or decorative glass jar with tight-fitting lid; cover.

For single serving: Place 1 cup apple cider and 1 heaping teaspoon spice mixture in small saucepan. Simmer cider mixture for 5 minutes. Strain before serving.

Put mixture in crock or attractive container and give with jug of country apple cider from your favorite farm stand or market. Include instructions for making spiced cider with the gift.

EASY COCOA MIX

2 cups nonfat dry milk powder
1 cup sugar
¾ cup powdered non-dairy creamer
½ cup unsweetened cocoa powder
¼ teaspoon salt

Combine all ingredients in small bowl until well blended. Spoon mixture into decorative gift jar; cover.

Makes about 4 cups mix or 16 servings

For single serving: Place rounded ¼ cup Easy Cocoa Mix in mug or cup; add ¾ cup boiling water. Stir until mix is dissolved. Top with sweetened whipped cream and marshmallows, if desired. Serve immediately.

Cocoa Marshmallow Mix: *Prepare Easy Cocoa Mix in 2-quart airtight container as directed, adding 1 package (10½ ounces) miniature marshmallows.*

For single serving: Place rounded ½ cup Cocoa Marshmallow Mix in mug or cup; add ¾ cup boiling water. Stir until mix is dissolved. Serve immediately.

MOCHA COFFEE MIX

1 cup nonfat dry milk powder
¾ cup granulated sugar
⅔ cup powdered non-dairy creamer
½ cup unsweetened cocoa powder
⅓ cup instant coffee, pressed through fine sieve
¼ cup packed brown sugar
1 teaspoon ground cinnamon
¼ teaspoon salt
¼ teaspoon ground nutmeg

Combine all ingredients in small bowl until well blended. Spoon mixture into decorative gift jar; cover.

Makes about 3½ cups mix or 10 to 12 servings

For single serving: Place rounded ¼ cup Mocha Coffee Mix in mug or cup; add ¾ cup boiling water. Stir until mix is dissolved. Serve immediately.

Left to right: Easy Cocoa Mix and Mocha Coffee Mix

YULETIDE BREADS AND MUFFINS

CHEDDAR PEPPER BREAD

Basic Yeast Bread (page 110)
2 cups cubed sharp Cheddar cheese
⅔ cup chopped red bell pepper
⅔ cup chopped green bell pepper
½ cup chopped onion
2 eggs
2 tablespoons water
Coarse salt (optional)

1. Prepare Basic Yeast Bread through Step 4. Grease baking sheets; set aside. Turn out dough onto lightly oiled work surface; divide in half.

2. Combine cheese, bell peppers and onion in medium bowl; divide in half. Knead half the pepper mixture into half the dough. Knead the other half of pepper mixture into other half of dough. Cover with towel on work surface; let rest 5 minutes.

3. Round each half of dough into a ball. Place on prepared baking sheets. Flatten each round of dough to about 2 inches thick. Cover with towel; let rise in warm place 45 minutes.

4. Beat eggs with water in small bowl. Lightly brush tops and sides of each loaf with egg mixture. Sprinkle tops of loaves with coarse salt, if desired.

5. Preheat oven to 375°F. Bake 30 minutes or until golden brown. Immediately remove loaves from baking sheets and allow to cool on wire rack. *Makes 2 loaves*

Cheddar Pepper Bread

Savory Pull-Apart Loaves

Basic Yeast Bread (recipe follows)
2 tablespoons dried basil
2 tablespoons rubbed sage
2 tablespoons dried thyme
2 tablespoons olive oil

1. Prepare Basic Yeast Bread through Step 5. Combine basil, sage and thyme in small bowl; set aside.

2. Divide half the dough into 16 equal pieces. Keep remaining half of dough covered. Form each piece into a ball. Cover with towel on work surface; let rest 5 minutes.

3. Flatten each ball into 4×3-inch oval. Coat both sides of dough with olive oil. Sprinkle one side of dough with rounded ½ teaspoon of herb mixture.

4. Stand loaf pan on short end. Lay one piece of dough, herb-covered side down, in pan. Stack remaining 15 pieces of dough in pan so that herb-covered sides of dough are touching sides of dough not covered with herb mixture. Cover with towel; let rise 45 minutes. Repeat with remaining half of dough.

5. Preheat oven to 375°F. Bake 35 minutes or until tops of loaves are golden. Immediately remove bread from pan and cool on wire rack. *Makes 2 loaves*

Basic Yeast Bread

2 cups milk
¼ cup unsalted butter, softened
6½ to 7½ cups all-purpose flour, divided
2 packages active dry yeast
2 teaspoons salt
¼ cup sugar
2 eggs

1. Heat milk and butter in small saucepan over medium heat just until butter is melted. Remove from heat; cool to about 120° to 130°F.

2. Combine 4 cups flour, yeast, salt and sugar in large bowl. Add milk mixture and eggs. Beat vigorously 2 minutes. Add remaining flour, ¼ cup at a time, until dough begins to pull away from sides of bowl.

3. Turn out dough onto lightly floured work surface; flatten slightly. Knead 10 minutes or until smooth and elastic, adding flour if necessary to prevent sticking.

4. Shape dough into a ball. Place in large lightly oiled bowl; turn dough over once to oil surface. Cover with towel; let rise in warm place about 1 hour or until doubled in bulk.

5. Grease two 9×5-inch loaf pans; set aside.

6. Turn out dough onto lightly oiled work surface; divide in half. Shape each half of dough into loaf; place in prepared pans. Cover with towel; let rise in warm place 45 minutes.

7. Preheat oven to 375°F. Bake 25 minutes or until loaves are golden and sound hollow when tapped. Immediately remove bread from pans and cool on wire rack.

Makes 2 loaves

Greek Flat Breads

Basic Yeast Bread (page 110)
1 cup chopped kalamata olives
½ pound crumbled feta cheese
6 cloves garlic, minced
2 tablespoons olive oil
2 eggs
2 tablespoons water
Coarse salt (optional)

1. Prepare Basic Yeast Bread through Step 4. Grease 2 baking sheets; set aside. Turn out dough onto lightly oiled work surface; divide in half. Keep remaining half of dough covered. Divide dough into 16 equal pieces. Form each piece into ball. Cover with towel on work surface; let rest 5 minutes.

2. Combine olives, cheese, garlic and oil in medium bowl; set aside.

3. Beat eggs with water in small bowl.

4. Flatten each ball of dough to ½-inch thickness. Place 2 inches apart on prepared baking sheet. Brush dough with beaten egg. Divide half the olive mixture into 16 equal portions. Sprinkle each round of dough with 1 portion of olive mixture; press topping into dough slightly.

5. Cover with towel; let rise 45 minutes. Repeat with remaining half of dough.

6. Place heavy pan on lower rack of oven. Preheat oven to 400°F.

7. Sprinkle tops of dough with coarse salt, if desired. Place bread in oven. Carefully place 4 to 5 ice cubes in heavy pan and place in oven. Close door immediately. Bake 15 minutes or until lightly browned. Immediately remove bread from baking sheets and place on wire rack to cool.

Makes 32 flat breads

Greek Flat Breads

113

CHEDDAR-ONION LOAF

1 cup water
1 package active dry yeast
2 teaspoons sugar
2 cups all-purpose flour
4 tablespoons butter,
    softened, divided
2 eggs
¼ teaspoon salt
1 cup whole wheat flour
1 large onion, finely chopped
4 ounces sharp Cheddar
    cheese, cut into ¼-inch
    pieces (about 1 cup)
½ teaspoon poppy seeds

HEAT water in small saucepan over low heat until temperature reaches 105° to 110°F. To proof yeast, sprinkle yeast and sugar over heated water in large bowl; stir until dissolved. Let stand 5 minutes or until mixture is bubbly. Add all-purpose flour, 2 tablespoons butter, eggs and salt. Beat with electric mixer at low speed until blended, scraping down side of bowl once. Increase speed to high; beat 10 minutes, scraping down side of bowl once. Stir in whole wheat flour with wooden spoon; stir until soft dough forms. Cover with plastic wrap; let rise in warm place 1 hour or until doubled in bulk. Meanwhile, cook onion in remaining 2 tablespoons butter in small skillet over medium heat about 4 minutes or until tender. Remove; set aside to cool.

SPRAY 9-inch pie plate with nonstick cooking spray. Sprinkle dough with cheese and half of onion. Stir dough with wooden spoon until cheese and onion are evenly distributed. Turn into pie plate. Spoon remaining onion over dough; sprinkle with poppy seeds. Let rise in warm place, uncovered, about 1 hour or until doubled in bulk.

PREHEAT oven to 375°F. Bake 30 minutes or until loaf sounds hollow when tapped. Remove immediately from pie plate. Cool on wire rack 30 minutes. *Makes 12 servings*

TOMATO AND CHEESE FOCACCIA

1 package active dry yeast
¾ cup warm water (105° to 115°F)
2 cups all-purpose flour
½ teaspoon salt
¼ cup olive oil, divided
1 teaspoon Italian seasoning
8 oil-packed sun-dried tomatoes, well drained
½ cup (2 ounces) shredded provolone cheese
¼ cup (1 ounce) freshly grated Parmesan cheese

Dissolve yeast in warm water; let stand 5 minutes. Combine flour and salt in work bowl of food processor.* Add yeast mixture and 3 tablespoons oil. Process until ingredients form a ball. Process 1 minute more. Turn out onto lightly floured surface. Knead about 2 minutes or until smooth and elastic. Place dough in oiled bowl; turn once to oil dough surface. Cover with kitchen towel. Let rise in warm place about 30 minutes or until doubled in bulk.

Punch dough down. Let rest 5 minutes. Press dough into oiled 10-inch cake pan, deep-dish pizza pan or springform pan. Brush with remaining 1 tablespoon oil. Sprinkle with Italian seasoning. Press sun-dried tomatoes around side of pan, about 1 inch from edge. Sprinkle with cheeses. Cover and let rise in warm place 15 minutes.

Preheat oven to 425°F. Bake 20 to 25 minutes or until golden brown. Cool completely in pan on wire rack. Carefully remove focaccia from pan. *Makes 1 (10-inch) bread*

If mixing dough by hand, combine flour and salt in large bowl. Stir in yeast mixture and 3 tablespoons oil until ingredients form a ball. Turn out onto lightly floured surface and knead about 10 minutes or until smooth and elastic. Proceed as directed.

Swedish Limpa Bread

Swedish Limpa Bread

¾ cup plus 4 teaspoons water, divided
2 tablespoons butter
¼ cup molasses, divided
1 teaspoon instant coffee granules
1¾ to 2 cups all-purpose flour, divided
½ cup rye flour
1 package active dry yeast
1 tablespoon sugar
1½ teaspoons grated orange peel
1 teaspoon salt
½ teaspoon fennel seeds, crushed
½ teaspoon caraway seeds, crushed
¼ teaspoon whole fennel seeds
¼ teaspoon whole caraway seeds

HEAT ¾ cup water, butter and 3 tablespoons molasses in small saucepan over low heat until temperature reaches 120° to 130°F. Stir in coffee. Combine 1½ cups all-purpose flour, rye flour, yeast, sugar, orange peel, salt and crushed seeds in large bowl. Stir heated water mixture into flour mixture with rubber spatula to form soft but sticky dough. Gradually add more all-purpose flour to form rough dough.

TURN out dough onto lightly floured surface. Knead 2 minutes or until soft dough forms, gradually adding remaining flour to prevent sticking, if necessary. Cover with inverted bowl; let rest 5 minutes. Continue kneading 5 to 8 minutes until smooth and elastic. Shape dough into ball; place in large greased bowl. Turn dough over so top is greased. Loosely cover with lightly greased sheet of plastic wrap. Let rise in warm place 75 minutes or until almost doubled in bulk.

PUNCH down dough. Grease 8½×4½-inch loaf pan. Roll dough into 12×7-inch rectangle. Starting with one short end, roll up tightly, jelly-roll style. Pinch seams and ends to seal. Place seam side down in prepared pan. Cover loosely; let rise in warm place 1 hour or until doubled in bulk.

PREHEAT oven to 350°F. Stir remaining 1 tablespoon molasses and remaining 4 teaspoons water in small bowl; set aside. Uncover loaf; make 3 diagonal slashes on top of dough using sharp knife. Bake 40 to 45 minutes or until loaf sounds hollow when tapped. Brush top with molasses mixture and sprinkle with whole seeds halfway through baking time. Brush again with molasses mixture about 10 minutes before removing loaf from oven. Cool in pan on wire rack 5 minutes. Remove from pan. Cool completely on wire rack.

Makes 12 servings

Chocolate Rolls

Basic Yeast Bread (page 110)
1 cup granulated sugar
6 tablespoons unsweetened cocoa powder, divided
1 teaspoon ground cinnamon
6 tablespoons butter, melted
2 cups powdered sugar
½ to ¾ cup heavy cream

A basket full of rich and gooey Chocolate Rolls is sure to spread holiday cheer!

1. Prepare Basic Yeast Bread through Step 4. Grease two 13×9×2-inch pans; set aside. Turn out dough onto lightly oiled work surface; divide in half. Roll half the dough into 20×15-inch rectangle. Keep remaining half of dough covered.

2. Combine granulated sugar, 4 tablespoons cocoa and cinnamon in small bowl.

3. Brush melted butter over dough, leaving ½-inch border on top short edge. Sprinkle half the sugar mixture over dough. Starting at short side; loosely roll up dough jelly-roll style. Using heavy thread or dental floss, cut dough in 12 equal slices. Place slices, cut side up, in prepared pan. Cover with towel; let rise 45 minutes. Repeat with remaining half of dough.

4. Preheat oven to 375°F. Bake 20 minutes or until golden brown. Allow rolls to cool in pan 30 minutes.

5. Combine powdered sugar, 2 tablespoons cocoa and 4 tablespoons cream in glass measuring cup. Add additional cream if necessary to reach desired consistency. Drizzle over tops of rolls. *Makes 24 rolls*

Chocolate Rolls

Sun-Dried Tomato and Basil Bread

1½–POUND LOAF INGREDIENTS
1 cup water
1½ tablespoons sugar
1½ teaspoons salt
2 teaspoons dried basil
    leaves
2 tablespoons olive oil
2 tablespoons toasted wheat
    germ
2¾ cups bread flour
¼ cup whole wheat flour
1½ teaspoons rapid-rise yeast
¼ cup oil-packed sun-dried
    tomatoes, drained and
    chopped

2–POUND LOAF INGREDIENTS
1½ cups water
2 tablespoons sugar
2 teaspoons salt
1 tablespoon dried basil
    leaves
3 tablespoons olive oil
3 tablespoons toasted wheat
    germ
3½ cups bread flour
½ cup whole wheat flour
2 teaspoons rapid-rise yeast
⅓ cup oil-packed sun-dried
    tomatoes, drained and
    chopped

PLACE all ingredients except tomatoes in bread machine pan in order specified by owner's manual. Spoon tomatoes into 4 corners of pan; do not cover yeast. Program basic cycle and desired crust setting; press start.

Makes 12 or 16 servings

Sun-Dried Tomato and Basil Bread

GARLIC AND HERB PARMESAN BUNS

8 BUNS INGREDIENTS
1¼ cups water
1 tablespoon sugar
1½ teaspoons salt
1 teaspoon garlic powder
2 teaspoons Italian herbs
⅓ cup grated Parmesan
     cheese
3 cups bread flour
1 tablespoon rapid-rise yeast

12 BUNS INGREDIENTS
1½ cups water
2 tablespoons sugar
2 teaspoons salt
1½ teaspoons garlic powder
1 tablespoon Italian herbs
½ cup grated Parmesan
     cheese
4 cups bread flour
1 tablespoon rapid-rise yeast

TOPPING:
1 to 2 tablespoons grated
     Parmesan cheese

PLACE all ingredients except topping in bread machine pan in order specified by owner's manual. Program dough cycle setting; press start.

TURN out dough onto lightly oiled surface. Cut dough into 8 pieces for small batch or 12 pieces for large batch. Shape into smooth balls. Place on greased baking sheet; flatten slightly. Let rise in warm place 45 minutes or until doubled.

PREHEAT oven to 400°F. Brush buns with water; sprinkle tops with pinch of cheese. Bake 15 minutes or until lightly browned. Serve warm or transfer onto wire rack to cool completely.   *Makes 8 or 12 buns*

Garlic and Herb Parmesan Buns

DILLED BUTTERMILK BREAD

1½–POUND LOAF INGREDIENTS
½ cup water
1 egg, lightly beaten
½ cup buttermilk*
1 tablespoon sugar
1 tablespoon butter
3 cups bread flour
1½ teaspoons dried dill weed
1 teaspoon salt
1½ teaspoons rapid-rise yeast

2–POUND LOAF INGREDIENTS
¾ cup water
1 egg, lightly beaten
¾ cup buttermilk*
2 tablespoons sugar
1½ tablespoons butter
4 cups bread flour
2 teaspoons dried dill weed
1½ teaspoons salt
2 teaspoons rapid-rise yeast

*You may substitute soured fresh milk. To sour milk, place 1 tablespoon lemon juice plus enough milk to equal 1 cup in 2-cup measure. Stir; let stand 5 minutes before using.

PLACE all ingredients in bread machine pan in order specified by owner's manual. Program basic cycle** and desired crust setting; press start.

Makes 12 or 16 servings

**For food safety reasons, this bread should not be baked on the delay-start cycle.

Dilled Buttermilk Bread

CARROT-RAISIN-NUT BREAD

1½–POUND LOAF INGREDIENTS
1 cup water
1 cup shredded carrots
2 tablespoons honey
1½ teaspoons salt
2 tablespoons butter
3 cups bread flour
¼ cup whole wheat flour
1½ teaspoons rapid-rise yeast
⅓ cup chopped walnuts
⅓ cup raisins

2–POUND LOAF INGREDIENTS
1¼ cups water
1½ cups shredded carrots
3 tablespoons honey
2 teaspoons salt
3 tablespoons butter
4 cups bread flour
⅓ cup whole wheat flour
2 teaspoons rapid-rise yeast
½ cup chopped walnuts
½ cup raisins

PLACE all ingredients except walnuts and raisins in bread machine pan in order specified by owner's manual. Program basic cycle and desired crust setting; press start. Add walnuts and raisins at the beep or at the end of first kneading cycle.

Makes 12 or 16 servings

Carrot-Raisin-Nut Bread

GERMAN RYE BEER BREAD

1½–POUND LOAF INGREDIENTS

1¼ cups room temperature
    beer
2 tablespoons light molasses
1 tablespoon butter
1½ teaspoons salt
2 teaspoons caraway seeds
2½ cups bread flour
½ cup rye flour
1½ teaspoons rapid-rise yeast

2–POUND LOAF INGREDIENTS

1½ cups room temperature
    beer
3 tablespoons light molasses
1½ tablespoons butter
2 teaspoons salt
1 tablespoon caraway seeds
3¼ cups bread flour
¾ cup rye flour
2 teaspoons rapid-rise yeast

PLACE all ingredients in bread machine pan in order specified by owner's manual. Program basic cycle and desired crust setting; press start.

Makes 12 or 16 servings

German Rye Beer Bread

TEX-MEX QUICK BREAD

1½ cups all-purpose flour
1 cup Monterey Jack cheese
½ cup cornmeal
½ cup sun-dried tomatoes, coarsely chopped
1 can (4.25 ounces) black olives, drained and chopped
¼ cup sugar
1½ teaspoons baking powder
1 teaspoon baking soda
1 cup milk
1 can (4.5 ounces) green chilies, drained and chopped
¼ cup olive oil
1 large egg, beaten

1. Preheat oven to 325°F. Grease 9×5-inch loaf pan or four 5×3-inch loaf pans; set aside.

2. Combine flour, cheese, cornmeal, tomatoes, olives, sugar, baking powder and baking soda in large bowl.

3. Combine milk, chilies, oil and egg in small bowl. Add to flour mixture; stir just until combined. Pour into prepared pan. Bake 9×5-inch loaf 45 minutes and 5×3-inch loaves 30 minutes or until toothpick inserted near center of loaf comes out clean. Cool in pan 15 minutes. Remove from pan and cool on wire rack.   *Makes 1 large loaf or 4 small loaves*

Muffin Variation: Preheat oven to 375°F. Spoon batter into 12 well-greased muffin cups. Bake 20 minutes or until toothpick inserted near center of muffin comes out clean.

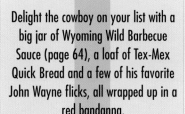

Delight the cowboy on your list with a big jar of Wyoming Wild Barbecue Sauce (page 64), a loaf of Tex-Mex Quick Bread and a few of his favorite John Wayne flicks, all wrapped up in a red bandanna.

Tex-Mex Quick Bread

SWEET POTATO BISCUITS

2½ cups all-purpose flour
¼ cup packed brown sugar
1 tablespoon baking powder
¾ teaspoon salt
¾ teaspoon ground cinnamon
¼ teaspoon ground ginger
¼ teaspoon ground allspice
½ cup vegetable shortening
½ cup chopped pecans
¾ cup mashed canned sweet
     potatoes
½ cup milk

Preheat oven to 450°F.

Combine flour, sugar, baking powder, salt, cinnamon, ginger and allspice in medium bowl. Cut in shortening with pastry blender or 2 knives until mixture resembles coarse crumbs. Stir in pecans.

Combine sweet potatoes and milk in separate medium bowl with wire whisk until smooth.

Make well in center of dry ingredients. Add sweet potato mixture; stir until mixture forms soft dough that clings together and forms a ball.

Turn out dough onto well-floured surface. Knead dough gently 10 to 12 times.

Roll or pat dough to ½-inch thickness. Cut out dough with floured 2½-inch biscuit cutter.

Place biscuits 2 inches apart on ungreased large baking sheet. Bake 12 to 14 minutes or until tops and bottoms are golden brown. *Makes about 12 biscuits*

Sweet Potato Biscuits

DILL SOUR CREAM SCONES

2 cups all-purpose flour
2 teaspoons baking powder
½ teaspoon baking soda
½ teaspoon salt
4 tablespoons butter
2 eggs
½ cup sour cream
1 tablespoon chopped fresh dill *or* 1 teaspoon dried dill weed

Preheat oven to 425°F.

Combine flour, baking powder, baking soda and salt. Cut in butter with pastry blender or 2 knives until mixture resembles coarse crumbs. Beat eggs with fork in small bowl. Add sour cream and dill; beat until well combined. Stir into flour mixture until mixture forms soft dough that pulls away from side of bowl.

Turn out dough onto well-floured surface. Knead dough 10 times. Roll out dough into 9×6-inch rectangle with lightly floured rolling pin. Cut dough into 6 (3-inch) squares. Cut each square diagonally in half, making 12 triangles. Place triangles 2 inches apart on ungreased baking sheets.

Bake 10 to 12 minutes or until golden brown and wooden pick inserted in center comes out clean. Cool on wire rack 10 minutes. Serve warm or cool completely.

Makes 12 scones

CAJUN BUBBLE BREAD

¼ cup (½ stick) unsalted
   butter
2 green onions, finely
   chopped
2 cloves garlic, minced
2 teaspoons Cajun seasoning
   spice blend*
4 tablespoons FRANK'S®
   Original REDHOT®
   Cayenne Pepper Sauce
¼ cup chopped almonds,
   divided
2 pounds frozen thawed
   bread dough
¾ cup (3 ounces) shredded
   Monterey Jack-Cheddar
   cheese blend, divided
2 tablespoons grated
   Parmesan cheese,
   divided

*If Cajun seasoning is
unavailable, substitute ¾
teaspoon each Italian seasoning
and chili powder, and ½
teaspoon celery seed.

1. Melt butter in small saucepan. Add onions, garlic and Cajun spice; cook over medium-low heat 3 minutes or just until tender. Remove from heat; stir in RedHot® sauce.

2. Grease 10-inch tube pan or 12-cup Bundt® pan.** Sprinkle bottom of tube pan with 1 tablespoon almonds. Cut bread dough into 24 (1-inch) pieces; shape into balls. Dip dough balls, one at a time, into butter mixture. Place in a single layer in bottom of tube pan. Sprinkle with ¼ cup Monterey Jack-Cheddar cheese, 1 tablespoon almonds and 2 teaspoons Parmesan.

3. Repeat layers twice with remaining ingredients. Cover with plastic wrap; let rise in warm place 1½ hours or until doubled in size.

4. Preheat oven to 375°F. Bake 35 minutes or until golden brown. (Loosely cover with foil during last 15 minutes if bread browns too quickly.) Loosen bread from sides of pan. Invert immediately onto serving plate; serve warm.

Makes 8 servings

**You may substitute 2 (8×4-inch) loaf pans.

Italian Herb Biscuit Loaf

ITALIAN HERB BISCUIT LOAF

1½ cups all-purpose flour
¼ cup grated Parmesan
    cheese
 2 tablespoons cornmeal
 2 teaspoons baking powder
½ teaspoon salt
¼ cup butter
 2 eggs
½ cup whipping cream
¾ teaspoon dried basil leaves
¾ teaspoon dried oregano
    leaves
⅛ teaspoon garlic powder
 Additional Parmesan cheese
    (optional)

PREHEAT oven to 425°F. Spray large cookie sheet with nonstick cooking spray; set aside.

COMBINE flour, cheese, cornmeal, baking powder and salt in large bowl. Cut in butter with pastry blender or 2 knives until mixture resembles coarse crumbs. Beat eggs in medium bowl. Add cream, basil, oregano and garlic powder; beat until well blended. Add cream mixture to flour mixture; stir until mixture forms ball.

TURN out dough onto well-floured surface. Knead 10 to 12 times; place on prepared cookie sheet. Roll or pat dough into 7-inch round, about 1 inch thick. Score top of dough into 8 wedges with tip of sharp knife; do not cut completely through dough. Sprinkle with additional cheese, if desired.

BAKE 20 to 25 minutes or until toothpick inserted into center comes out clean. Cool on cookie sheet on wire rack 10 minutes. Serve warm. *Makes 8 servings*

PESTO SURPRISE MUFFINS

2 cups all-purpose flour
3 tablespoons grated
    Parmesan cheese,
    divided
1 tablespoon baking powder
½ teaspoon salt
1 cup milk
¼ cup vegetable oil
1 egg
¼ cup prepared pesto sauce

PREHEAT oven to 400°F. Grease 12 (2½-inch) muffin cups.

COMBINE flour, 2 tablespoons cheese, baking powder and salt in large bowl. Whisk together milk, oil and egg in small bowl until blended. Stir into flour mixture just until moistened. Spoon into prepared muffin cups, filling ⅓ full. Stir pesto sauce; spoon 1 teaspoon sauce into each muffin cup. Spoon remaining batter evenly over pesto sauce. Sprinkle remaining 1 tablespoon cheese evenly over muffins.

BAKE 25 to 30 minutes or until toothpick inserted into centers comes out clean. Cool in muffin pan on wire rack 5 minutes. Remove from pan and cool on wire rack.

Makes 12 muffins

ONION-WHEAT PAN BREAD

⅓ cup wheat germ, divided
1¾ cups all-purpose flour
2 tablespoons sugar
1¾ teaspoons baking powder
½ teaspoon salt
1 cup milk
⅓ cup finely chopped green
    onions
⅓ cup vegetable oil
1 egg
2 tablespoons grated
    Parmesan cheese
1 tablespoon toasted sesame
    seeds

PREHEAT oven to 400°F. Spray 9-inch cast iron skillet with nonstick cooking spray.* Heat skillet in oven 5 minutes. Reserve 1 tablespoon wheat germ; set aside.

COMBINE remaining wheat germ, flour, sugar, baking powder and salt in large bowl. Beat milk, onions, oil and egg in medium bowl with fork. Add to flour mixture; stir just until moistened. Spoon into preheated skillet. Sprinkle with reserved wheat germ, cheese and sesame seeds.

BAKE 15 minutes or until golden brown and toothpick inserted into center comes out clean. Cool on wire rack.

Makes 12 servings

*You can substitute 9-inch round pan sprayed with nonstick cooking spray. Do not preheat pan in oven. Increase baking time to 20 minutes.

Pesto Surprise Muffins

WHEAT GERM BREAD

¾ cup wheat germ, divided
¾ cup all-purpose flour
½ cup whole wheat flour
¼ cup packed light brown
    sugar
1 teaspoon baking soda
½ teaspoon baking powder
¼ teaspoon salt
½ cup raisins
1 cup buttermilk*
4 tablespoons butter, melted
1 egg

*You may substitute soured fresh milk. To sour milk, place 1 tablespoon lemon juice plus enough milk to equal 1 cup in 2-cup measure. Stir; let stand 5 minutes before using.

PREHEAT oven to 350°F. Spray 8½×4½-inch loaf pan with nonstick cooking spray; set aside. Measure 2 tablespoons wheat germ; set aside.

COMBINE remaining wheat germ, all-purpose flour, whole wheat flour, sugar, baking soda, baking powder and salt in large bowl. Add raisins; stir until coated. Beat buttermilk, butter and egg in small bowl with fork. Stir into flour mixture. Pour into prepared pan. Sprinkle with reserved 2 tablespoons wheat germ.

BAKE 40 to 50 minutes or until toothpick inserted into center comes out clean. Cool in pan on wire rack 10 minutes. Remove from pan and cool 30 minutes on wire rack.

Makes 12 servings

Wheat Germ Bread

APRICOT-CRANBERRY HOLIDAY BREAD

⅔ cup milk

6 tablespoons butter, softened

2½ to 3 cups all-purpose flour, divided

4 tablespoons sugar

1 package active dry yeast

¾ teaspoon salt

½ teaspoon ground ginger

½ teaspoon ground nutmeg

2 eggs, divided

½ cup dried apricots, chopped

½ cup dried cranberries, chopped

3 tablespoons orange juice

½ cup pecans, toasted and coarsely chopped

1 teaspoon water

HEAT milk and butter in saucepan over low heat until temperature reaches 120° to 130°F. Combine 1½ cups flour, sugar, yeast, salt, ginger and nutmeg in bowl. Slowly add heated milk mixture to flour mixture. Add 1 egg; stir with rubber spatula 2 minutes or until blended. Gradually add more flour until dough begins to lose its stickiness, about 2 to 3 minutes. Mix apricots, cranberries and orange juice in small microwavable bowl; cover with plastic wrap. Microwave at HIGH 25 to 35 seconds to soften; set aside.

TURN out dough onto floured surface. Knead 5 to 8 minutes or until smooth and elastic; gradually add remaining flour to prevent sticking, if necessary. Drain or blot apricot mixture. Combine apricot mixture and pecans in bowl. Flatten dough into ¾-inch-thick rectangle; sprinkle with ⅓ fruit mixture. Roll up jelly-roll style from short end. Flatten dough; repeat twice using remaining fruit mixture. Continue to knead until blended. Shape dough into ball; place in large greased bowl. Turn dough over. Cover; let rise 1 hour or until doubled.

GREASE 9-inch cake or pie pan. Punch down dough; pat into 8-inch circle. Place in pan. Loosely cover with lightly greased sheet of plastic wrap. Let rise 1 hour or until doubled in size.

PREHEAT oven to 375°F. Beat remaining egg with 1 teaspoon water in small bowl; brush evenly over dough. Bake 30 to 35 minutes or until loaf sounds hollow when tapped. Remove immediately from pan. Cool completely on wire rack.

Makes 12 servings

Apricot-Cranberry Holiday Bread

Festive Yule Loaves

2¾ cups all-purpose flour,
    divided
⅓ cup sugar
1 teaspoon salt
1 package active dry yeast
1 cup milk
½ cup butter
1 egg
½ cup golden raisins
½ cup chopped candied red
    and green cherries
½ cup chopped pecans
    Vanilla Glaze (recipe
    follows), optional

Combine 1½ cups flour, sugar, salt and yeast in large bowl. Heat milk and butter over medium heat until very warm (120° to 130°F). Gradually stir into flour mixture. Add egg. Mix with electric mixer on low speed 1 minute. Beat on high speed 3 minutes, scraping sides of bowl frequently. Toss raisins, cherries and pecans with ¼ cup flour in small bowl; stir into yeast mixture. Stir in enough of remaining 1 cup flour to make a soft dough. Turn out onto lightly floured surface. Knead about 10 minutes or until smooth and elastic. Place in greased bowl; turn to grease top of dough. Cover with towel. Let rise in warm, draft-free place about 1 hour or until double in volume.

Punch dough down. Divide in half. Roll out each half on lightly floured surface to form 8-inch circle. Fold in half; press only folded edge firmly. Place on ungreased cookie sheet. Cover with towel. Let rise in warm, draft-free place about 30 minutes or until double in volume.

Preheat oven to 375°F. Bake 20 to 25 minutes until golden brown. Remove from cookie sheet and cool completely on wire rack. Frost with Vanilla Glaze, if desired. Store in airtight containers.   *Makes 2 loaves*

Vanilla Glaze:

Combine 1 cup sifted powdered sugar, 4 to 5 teaspoons light cream or half-and-half and ½ teaspoon vanilla extract in small bowl; stir until smooth.

Festive Yule Loaf

145

MAPLE-PUMPKIN-PECAN TWIST

1 can (15 ounces) pumpkin
1 cup water
½ cup vegetable shortening
7 to 8 cups all-purpose flour, divided
2 cups pecans, coarsely chopped
½ cup sugar
2 packages active dry yeast
2 teaspoons salt
2 large eggs
2 teaspoons maple flavoring, divided
6 to 8 tablespoons milk
2 cups powdered sugar

1. Heat pumpkin, water and shortening in medium saucepan over medium heat until shortening is melted and temperature reaches 120° to 130°F. Remove from heat.

2. Combine 4 cups flour, pecans, sugar, yeast and salt in large bowl. Add pumpkin mixture, eggs and 1 teaspoon maple flavoring; beat vigorously 2 minutes. Add remaining flour, ¼ cup at a time, until dough begins to pull away from sides of bowl. Turn out dough onto lightly floured work surface; flatten slightly. Knead 10 minutes or until smooth and elastic, adding flour if necessary to prevent sticking. Shape dough into ball. Place in large lightly oiled bowl; turn dough over once to oil surface. Cover with towel; let rise in warm place about 1 hour or until doubled in bulk.

3. Turn out dough onto lightly oiled work surface; divide into four pieces. Shape each piece into 24-inch-long rope. Lightly twist two of the ropes together. Join ends to form ring. Tuck ends under loaf to prevent untwisting. Place on lightly oiled baking sheet. Repeat with remaining two ropes. Cover with towel; let rise in warm place 45 minutes.

4. Preheat oven to 375°F. Bake 25 minutes or until deep golden brown. Immediately remove bread from baking sheets and cool on wire rack 20 minutes.

5. Combine remaining 1 teaspoon maple flavoring and 6 tablespoons milk in small bowl. Whisk milk mixture and powdered sugar together in medium bowl. If icing is too thick, add remaining milk, 1 teaspoon at a time, to reach desired consistency. Drizzle over loaves in zigzag pattern.

Makes 2 large twists

Maple-Pumpkin-Pecan Twist

HOLIDAY STOLLEN

1½ cups unsalted butter, softened
4 egg yolks
½ cup granulated sugar
1 teaspoon salt
Grated peel from 1 lemon
Grated peel from 1 orange
1 teaspoon vanilla
2½ cups hot milk (120° to 130°F)
8 to 8½ cups all-purpose flour, divided
2 packages active dry yeast
½ cup *each* golden raisins, candied orange peel, candied lemon peel, chopped candied red cherries, chopped candied green cherries and chopped almonds
1 egg, beaten
Powdered sugar

Beat butter, egg yolks, granulated sugar, salt, lemon peel, orange peel and vanilla in large bowl until light and fluffy. Slowly add milk; mix thoroughly. Add 2 cups flour and yeast; mix well. When mixture is smooth, add enough remaining flour, ½ cup at a time, until dough forms and can be lifted out of bowl. Lightly flour work surface; knead dough until smooth and elastic, about 10 minutes. Mix raisins, candied orange and lemon peels, cherries and almonds in medium bowl; knead fruit mixture into dough.

Place dough in greased bowl, cover with plastic wrap and let rise in warm place until doubled in bulk, about 1 hour.

Grease 2 large baking sheets. Turn dough out onto floured work surface. Divide dough in half. Place one half back in bowl; cover and set aside. Cut remaining half into thirds. Roll each third into 12-inch rope. Place on prepared baking sheet. Braid ropes together. Repeat procedure with remaining dough.

Brush beaten egg on braids. Let braids stand at room temperature until doubled in bulk, about 1 hour.

Preheat oven to 350°F. Bake until braids are golden brown and sound hollow when tapped, about 45 minutes. Remove to wire rack to cool. Sprinkle with powdered sugar before serving.   *Makes 2 braided loaves*

Holiday Stollen

Peanut Butter Chocolate Chip Loaves

3 cups all-purpose flour
1½ teaspoons baking powder
1 teaspoon baking soda
1 teaspoon salt
1 cup creamy peanut butter
½ cup butter, softened
½ cup granulated sugar
½ cup packed light brown
    sugar
2 eggs
1½ cups buttermilk*
2 teaspoons vanilla
1 cup semisweet mini
    chocolate chips

*You may substitute soured fresh milk. To sour milk, place 4½ teaspoons lemon juice plus enough milk to equal 1½ cups in 2-cup measure. Stir; let stand 5 minutes before using.

PREHEAT oven to 350°F. Spray two 8½×4½-inch loaf pans with nonstick cooking spray; set aside.

SIFT flour, baking powder, baking soda and salt into large bowl; set aside. Beat peanut butter, butter, granulated sugar and brown sugar in another large bowl with electric mixer at medium speed until light and fluffy. Beat in eggs, 1 at a time, scraping down side of bowl after each addition. Beat in buttermilk and vanilla. Gradually add flour mixture. Beat at low speed. Stir in chocolate chips; divide batter evenly between prepared pans.

BAKE 45 minutes or until toothpick inserted into centers comes out clean. Cool in pans on wire racks 10 minutes. Remove from pans and cool completely on wire racks.

Makes 24 servings

Variation: Stir in ¾ cup chocolate chips before baking; sprinkle with remaining ¼ cup after baking.

Peanut Butter Chocolate Chip Loaf

151

PUMPKIN STREUSEL COFFEE CAKE

STREUSEL TOPPING
- ½ cup all-purpose flour
- ¼ cup packed brown sugar
- 1½ teaspoons ground cinnamon
- 3 tablespoons butter or margarine
- ½ cup coarsely chopped nuts

COFFEE CAKE
- 2 cups all-purpose flour
- 2 teaspoons baking powder
- 1½ teaspoons ground cinnamon
- ½ teaspoon baking soda
- ¼ teaspoon salt
- 1 cup (2 sticks) butter or margarine, softened
- 1 cup granulated sugar
- 2 eggs
- 1 cup LIBBY'S® Solid Pack Pumpkin
- 1 teaspoon vanilla extract

FOR STREUSEL TOPPING:
COMBINE flour, brown sugar and cinnamon in medium bowl. Cut in butter with pastry blender or two knives until mixture is crumbly; stir in nuts.

FOR COFFEE CAKE:
COMBINE flour, baking powder, cinnamon, baking soda and salt in small bowl. Beat butter and sugar in large mixing bowl until creamy. Add eggs one at a time, beating well after each addition. Beat in pumpkin and vanilla extract. Gradually beat in flour mixture.

SPOON *half* of batter into greased and floured 9-inch round cake pan. Sprinkle ¾ *cup* Streusel Topping over batter. Spoon *remaining* batter evenly over Streusel Topping; sprinkle with *remaining* Streusel Topping.

BAKE in preheated 350°F. oven for 45 to 50 minutes or until wooden pick inserted in center comes out clean. Cool in pan on wire rack for 10 minutes; remove to wire rack to cool completely. *Makes 10 servings*

CHOCOLATE CHUNK COFFEE CAKE

NUT LAYER:
- 1 package (4 ounces) BAKER'S® GERMAN'S Sweet Chocolate, chopped
- ½ cup chopped nuts
- ¼ cup sugar
- 1 teaspoon cinnamon

CAKE:
- 1¾ cups all-purpose flour
- ½ teaspoon CALUMET® Baking Powder
- ¼ teaspoon salt
- 1 cup (½ pint) sour cream or plain yogurt
- 1 teaspoon baking soda
- ½ cup (1 stick) margarine or butter, softened
- 1 cup sugar
- 2 eggs
- ½ teaspoon vanilla

HEAT oven to 350°F.

MIX chocolate, nuts, ¼ cup sugar and cinnamon; set aside. Mix flour, baking powder and salt; set aside. Combine sour cream and baking soda; set aside.

BEAT margarine and 1 cup sugar in large bowl until light and fluffy. Add eggs, one at a time, beating well after each addition. Add vanilla. Add flour mixture alternately with sour cream mixture, beginning and ending with flour mixture. Spoon ½ the batter into greased 9-inch square pan. Top with ½ the chocolate-nut mixture, spreading carefully with spatula. Repeat layers.

BAKE for 30 to 35 minutes or until cake begins to pull away from sides of pan. Cool in pan; cut into squares.

Makes 9 servings

Sour Cream Coffee Cake with Chocolate and Walnuts

SOUR CREAM COFFEE CAKE WITH CHOCOLATE AND WALNUTS

¾ **cup butter, softened**
1½ **cups packed light brown sugar**
3 **eggs**
2 **teaspoons vanilla**
3 **cups all-purpose flour**
2 **teaspoons baking powder**
2 **teaspoons ground cinnamon**
1½ **teaspoons baking soda**
½ **teaspoon ground nutmeg**
¼ **teaspoon salt**
1½ **cups sour cream**
½ **cup semisweet chocolate chips**
½ **cup chopped walnuts**
   Powdered sugar

Preheat oven to 350°F. Grease and flour 12-cup Bundt® pan or 10-inch tube pan. Beat butter in large bowl with electric mixer on medium speed until creamy. Add brown sugar; beat until light and fluffy. Beat in eggs and vanilla until well blended. Combine flour, baking powder, cinnamon, baking soda, nutmeg and salt in large bowl; add to butter mixture on low speed alternately with sour cream, beginning and ending with flour mixture until well blended. Stir in chocolate and walnuts. Spoon into prepared pan.

Bake 45 to 50 minutes until wooden pick inserted in center comes out clean. Cool in pan 15 minutes. Remove from pan to wire rack; cool completely. Store tightly covered at room temperature. Sprinkle with powdered sugar before serving.

Makes one coffee cake

2½ cups all-purpose flour
¾ cup sugar
½ teaspoon baking powder
½ teaspoon baking soda
2 packages (3 ounces each)
    cream cheese, softened,
    divided
¾ cup milk
2 tablespoons vegetable oil
2 eggs, divided
1 teaspoon vanilla
½ cup flaked coconut
¾ cup cherry preserves
2 tablespoons butter

CHERRY-COCONUT-CHEESE COFFEE CAKE

PREHEAT oven to 350°F. Grease and flour 9-inch springform pan. Combine flour and sugar in large bowl. Reserve ½ cup flour mixture; set aside. Stir baking powder and baking soda into remaining flour mixture. Cut in 1 package cream cheese with pastry blender or 2 knives until mixture resembles coarse crumbs; set aside.

COMBINE milk, oil and 1 egg in medium bowl. Add to cream cheese mixture; stir just until moistened. Spread batter on bottom and 1 inch up side of prepared pan. Combine remaining package cream cheese, remaining egg and vanilla in small bowl; stir until smooth. Pour over batter, spreading to within 1 inch of edge. Sprinkle coconut over cream cheese mixture. Spoon preserves evenly over coconut.

CUT butter into reserved flour mixture with pastry blender or 2 knives until mixture resembles coarse crumbs. Sprinkle over preserves. Bake 55 to 60 minutes or until brown and toothpick inserted into crust comes out clean. Cool in pan on wire rack 15 minutes. Remove side of pan; serve warm.

Makes 10 servings

Cherry-Coconut-Cheese Coffee Cake

WALNUT-CHOCOLATE QUICK BREAD

1½ cups milk
1 cup sugar
⅓ cup vegetable oil
1 egg, beaten
1 tablespoon molasses
1 teaspoon vanilla
3 cups all-purpose flour
3 tablespoons unsweetened
    cocoa powder
2 teaspoons baking soda
2 teaspoons baking powder
1 teaspoon salt
1 cup chocolate chips
½ cup walnuts, coarsely
    chopped

1. Preheat oven to 350°F. Grease four 5×3-inch loaf pans; set aside.

2. Combine milk, sugar, oil, egg, molasses and vanilla in medium bowl. Stir until sugar is dissolved; set aside.

3. Whisk together flour, cocoa, baking soda, baking powder and salt in large bowl. Add chocolate chips, nuts and sugar mixture; stir just until combined. Pour into prepared pans.

4. Bake 30 minutes or until toothpick inserted near center of loaf comes out clean. Cool in pan 15 minutes. Remove from pan and cool on wire rack. *Makes 4 loaves*

Muffin Variation: Preheat oven to 375°F. Spoon batter into 12 greased muffin cups. Bake 20 minutes or until toothpick inserted near center of muffin comes out clean.

Create a chocolate-lover's gift basket. Begin with a loaf of Walnut-Chocolate Quick Bread. Add a decorative tin of Double Chocolate Fantasy Bars (page 262) and a jar of Chocolate-Cherry Chutney (page 88) to the basket. For the finishing touch, sprinkle with individually wrapped Black and White Caramels (page 358).

Walnut-Chocolate Quick Bread

CRANBERRY RAISIN NUT BREAD

1½ cups all-purpose flour
¾ cup packed light brown
    sugar
1½ teaspoons baking powder
½ teaspoon baking soda
½ teaspoon ground cinnamon
½ teaspoon ground nutmeg
1 cup halved fresh or frozen
    cranberries
½ cup golden raisins
½ cup coarsely chopped
    pecans
1 tablespoon grated orange
    peel
2 eggs
¾ cup milk
3 tablespoons butter, melted
1 teaspoon vanilla extract
    Cranberry-Orange Spread
    (recipe follows), optional

Preheat oven to 350°F. Grease 8½×4½-inch loaf pan.

Combine flour, brown sugar, baking powder, baking soda, cinnamon and nutmeg in large bowl. Stir in cranberries, raisins, pecans and orange peel. Mix eggs, milk, melted butter and vanilla in small bowl until combined; stir into flour mixture just until moistened. Spoon into prepared pan.

Bake 55 to 60 minutes or until wooden toothpick inserted in center comes out clean. Cool in pan 15 minutes. Remove from pan and cool completely on wire rack. Store tightly wrapped in plastic wrap at room temperature. Serve with Cranberry-Orange Spread, if desired. *Makes 1 loaf*

CRANBERRY-ORANGE SPREAD

1 package (8 ounces) cream cheese, softened
1 package (3 ounces) cream cheese, softened
1 container (12 ounces) cranberry-orange sauce
¾ cup chopped pecans

Combine cream cheese and cranberry-orange sauce in small bowl. Stir with spoon until blended. Stir in pecans. Store in refrigerator. *Makes about 3 cups spread*

Cranberry Raisin Nut Bread

161

APPLESAUCE-SPICE BREAD

1½ cups all-purpose flour
1 cup unsweetened applesauce
¾ cup packed light brown sugar
¼ cup shortening
1 egg
1 teaspoon vanilla
¾ teaspoon baking soda
¾ teaspoon ground cinnamon
¼ teaspoon baking powder
¼ teaspoon salt
¼ teaspoon ground nutmeg
½ cup toasted chopped walnuts
½ cup raisins (optional)
Powdered sugar

PREHEAT oven to 350°F. Spray 9×9-inch baking pan with nonstick cooking spray; set aside.

BEAT flour, applesauce, brown sugar, shortening, egg, vanilla, baking soda, cinnamon, baking powder, salt and nutmeg in large bowl with electric mixer at low speed 30 seconds, scraping down side of bowl once. Increase speed to high; beat 3 minutes, scraping down side of bowl once. Stir in walnuts and raisins, if desired. Pour into prepared pan.

BAKE 30 minutes until brown and toothpick inserted into center comes out clean. Cool in pan on wire rack. Sprinkle with powdered sugar.

Makes 9 servings

Applesauce-Spice Bread

DATE NUT BREAD

2 cups all-purpose flour
½ cup packed light brown
    sugar
1 tablespoon baking powder
½ teaspoon salt
¼ cup butter
1 cup toasted chopped
    walnuts
1 cup chopped dates
1¼ cups milk
1 egg
½ teaspoon grated lemon peel

PREHEAT oven to 375°F. Spray 9×5-inch loaf pan with nonstick cooking spray; set aside.

COMBINE flour, sugar, baking powder and salt in large bowl. Cut in butter with pastry blender or 2 knives until mixture resembles fine crumbs. Add walnuts and dates; stir until coated. Beat milk, egg and lemon peel in small bowl with fork. Add to flour mixture; stir until moistened. Pour into prepared pan.

BAKE 45 to 50 minutes or until toothpick inserted into center comes out clean. Cool in pan on wire rack 10 minutes. Remove from pan and cool completely on wire rack.

Makes 12 servings

PIÑA COLADA BREAD

2½ cups flour
½ cup sugar
2 teaspoons baking powder
½ teaspoon baking soda
½ teaspoon salt
2 eggs
½ cup KARO® Light Corn
    Syrup
⅓ cup MAZOLA® Corn Oil
¼ cup rum
1 can (8 ounces) crushed
    pineapple in
    unsweetened juice,
    undrained
1 cup flaked coconut

1. Preheat oven to 350°F. Grease and flour 9×5×3-inch loaf pan.

2. In medium bowl, combine flour, sugar, baking powder, baking soda and salt. In large bowl, with mixer at medium speed, beat eggs, corn syrup, corn oil and rum until blended. Gradually stir in flour mixture just until moistened. Stir in pineapple with juice and coconut. Pour into prepared pan.

3. Bake 60 to 65 minutes or until toothpick inserted in center comes out clean. Cool in pan 10 minutes. Remove from pan; cool on wire rack.

Makes 1 loaf

Date Nut Bread

Pumpkin-Pecan Friendship Bread

3 cups chopped pecans, divided
1 can (16 ounces) solid-pack pumpkin
1 cup Starter (recipe follows)
4 eggs
½ cup vegetable oil
2 teaspoons vanilla
3 cups all-purpose flour
1 cup granulated sugar
1 cup packed light brown sugar
4 teaspoons ground cinnamon
2 teaspoons baking powder
1 teaspoon baking soda
1 teaspoon ground nutmeg
1 teaspoon ground ginger
1 teaspoon ground cloves

1. Preheat oven to 350°F. Grease and flour 2 (9½×4-inch) loaf pans. Set aside.

2. Reserve 1 cup pecans. Spread remaining 2 cups pecans in single layer in large baking pan. Bake 8 minutes or until golden brown, stirring frequently.

3. Combine pumpkin, Starter, eggs, oil and vanilla in large bowl. Combine remaining ingredients in separate large bowl until well blended. Stir into pumpkin mixture just until blended. Stir in toasted pecans. Spoon batter evenly into prepared pans. Sprinkle reserved pecans evenly over batter.

4. Bake 1 hour or until wooden pick inserted in centers comes out clean. Cool in pans on wire rack 5 minutes. Remove from pans. Cool completely on wire rack.

Makes 2 loaves

Starter

1 cup sugar
1 cup all-purpose flour
1 cup milk

1. Combine all ingredients in large resealable plastic food storage bag. Knead bag until well blended. Let bag stand at room temperature 5 days. Knead bag 5 times each day.

2. On day 6, add 1 cup sugar, 1 cup flour and 1 cup milk. Knead bag until well blended. Let stand at room temperature 4 days. Knead bag 5 times each day.

3. On day 10, pour 1 cup Starter into each of 3 bags. Reserve remaining 1 cup starter for recipe. Give remaining bags of starters with recipes as gifts.   *Makes about 4 cups*

Banana Bran Loaf

1 cup mashed ripe bananas
   (about 2 large)
½ cup granulated sugar
⅓ cup margarine, melted
⅓ cup skim milk
2 egg whites, slightly beaten
1¼ cups all-purpose flour
1 cup QUAKER® Oat Bran hot
   cereal, uncooked
2 teaspoons baking powder
½ teaspoon baking soda

Heat oven to 350°F. Lightly spray 8×4-inch or 9×5-inch loaf pan with nonstick cooking spray or oil lightly. Combine bananas, sugar, melted margarine, milk and egg whites; mix well. Add combined flour, oat bran, baking powder and baking soda, mixing just until moistened. Pour into prepared pan. Bake 55 to 60 minutes or until wooden toothpick inserted in center comes out clean. Cool 10 minutes; remove from pan. Cool completely on wire rack.

Makes 1 loaf (16 servings)

Orchard Fruit Bread

3 cups all-purpose flour or
   oat flour blend
⅔ cup sugar
1 teaspoon baking soda
2 eggs, beaten
1 carton (8 ounces) lemon
   lowfat yogurt
⅓ cup vegetable oil
1 teaspoon grated lemon peel
1 can (15 ounces) DEL
   MONTE® LITE® Fruit
   Cocktail, drained
½ cup chopped walnuts or
   pecans

1. Preheat oven to 350°F. Combine flour, sugar and baking soda; mix well.

2. Blend eggs with yogurt, oil and lemon peel. Add to dry ingredients along with fruit cocktail and nuts; stir just enough to blend. Spoon into greased 9×5-inch loaf pan.

3. Bake 60 to 70 minutes or until wooden pick inserted into center comes out clean. Let stand in pan 10 minutes. Turn out onto wire rack; cool completely.

Makes 1 loaf

Caramel Pecan Spice Cakes

CARAMEL PECAN SPICE CAKES

CAKE

1 package Duncan Hines® Moist Deluxe® Spice Cake Mix

1 package (4-serving size) vanilla instant pudding and pie filling mix

4 eggs

1 cup water

⅓ cup Crisco® Oil

1½ cups pecan pieces, toasted and finely chopped

CARAMEL GLAZE

3 tablespoons butter or margarine

3 tablespoons brown sugar

3 tablespoons granulated sugar

3 tablespoons whipping cream

½ cup confectioners sugar

¼ teaspoon vanilla extract

Pecan halves, for garnish

Maraschino cherry halves, for garnish

1. Preheat oven to 350°F. Grease and flour two 8½×4½×2½-inch loaf pans.

2. For cake, combine cake mix, pudding mix, eggs, water and oil in large bowl. Beat at medium speed with electric mixer for 2 minutes. Stir in toasted pecans. Pour batter into pans. Bake at 350°F for 55 to 60 minutes or until toothpick inserted in center comes out clean. Cool in pans 15 minutes. Loosen loaves from pans. Invert onto cooling rack. Turn right sides up. Cool completely.

3. For caramel glaze, combine butter, brown sugar, granulated sugar and whipping cream in small heavy saucepan. Bring to a boil on medium heat; boil 1 minute. Remove from heat; cool 20 minutes. Add confectioners sugar and vanilla extract; blend with wooden spoon until smooth and thick. Spread evenly on cooled loaves. Garnish with pecan halves and maraschino cherry halves before glaze sets.

Makes 2 loaves

CHOCOLATE-RASPBERRY LOAF

1 cup semisweet chocolate
chips
4 tablespoons butter
2 cups all-purpose flour
½ cup sugar
1 teaspoon baking soda
½ teaspoon baking powder
¼ teaspoon salt
1 cup toasted finely chopped
walnuts
2 eggs
¾ cup milk
½ cup seedless raspberry
spreadable fruit
1 teaspoon vanilla

PREHEAT oven to 350°F. Spray 9×5-inch loaf pan with nonstick cooking spray; set aside. Melt chocolate chips and butter in small saucepan over low heat; set aside.

COMBINE flour, sugar, baking soda, baking powder and salt in large bowl. Add walnuts; stir well. Lightly beat eggs in medium bowl with wire whisk. Add milk, spreadable fruit and vanilla. Beat until well blended. Add chocolate and milk mixtures to flour mixture. Stir just until moistened. Pour into prepared pan.

BAKE 50 to 60 minutes or until toothpick inserted into center comes out clean. Cool in pan on wire rack 10 minutes. Remove from pan; cool completely.   *Makes 12 servings*

CHERRY EGGNOG QUICK BREAD

2½ cups all-purpose flour
¾ cup sugar
1 tablespoon baking powder
½ teaspoon ground nutmeg
1¼ cups prepared dairy eggnog
6 tablespoons butter, melted
and cooled
2 eggs, slightly beaten
1 teaspoon vanilla
½ cup chopped pecans
½ cup chopped candied red
cherries

Preheat oven to 350°F. Grease three 5½×3-inch mini-loaf pans.

Combine flour, sugar, baking powder and nutmeg in large bowl. Stir eggnog, melted butter, eggs and vanilla in medium bowl until well blended. Add eggnog mixture to flour mixture. Mix just until all ingredients are moistened. Stir in pecans and cherries. Spoon into prepared pans.

Bake 35 to 40 minutes or until wooden toothpick inserted in centers comes out clean. Cool in pans 15 minutes. Remove from pans and cool completely on wire rack. Store tightly wrapped in plastic wrap at room temperature.

Makes 3 mini loaves

Chocolate-Raspberry Loaf

Pecan Streusel Topping
(recipe follows)
1½ cups all-purpose flour
½ cup sugar
2 teaspoons baking powder
½ cup milk
½ cup butter, melted and
   cooled
1 egg, beaten
1 cup fresh or individually
   frozen, whole unsugared
   raspberries

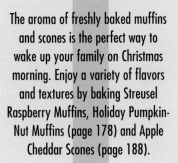

The aroma of freshly baked muffins and scones is the perfect way to wake up your family on Christmas morning. Enjoy a variety of flavors and textures by baking Streusel Raspberry Muffins, Holiday Pumpkin-Nut Muffins (page 178) and Apple Cheddar Scones (page 188).

STREUSEL RASPBERRY MUFFINS

Preheat oven to 375°F. Grease or paper-line 12 (2½-inch) muffin cups. Prepare Pecan Streusel Topping; set aside.

Combine flour, sugar and baking powder in large bowl. Combine milk, butter and egg in small bowl until blended. Stir into flour mixture just until moistened. Spoon half of batter into muffin cups. Divide raspberries among cups, then top with remaining batter. Sprinkle Pecan Streusel Topping over tops. Bake 25 to 30 minutes or until golden and wooden pick inserted in center comes out clean. Remove from pan.

Makes 12 muffins

PECAN STREUSEL TOPPING:

In small bowl, combine ¼ cup *each* chopped pecans, packed brown sugar and all-purpose flour. Stir in 2 tablespoons melted butter or margarine until mixture resembles moist crumbs.

Streusel Raspberry Muffins

173

CRANBERRY CHEESECAKE MUFFINS

1 package (3 ounces) cream cheese, softened
¼ cup sugar, divided
1 cup 2% milk
⅓ cup vegetable oil
1 egg
1 package (15.6 ounces) cranberry quick bread mix

1. Preheat oven to 400°F. Grease 12 muffin cups.

2. Beat cream cheese and 2 tablespoons sugar in small bowl until well blended. Combine milk, oil and egg in large bowl; beat with fork until blended. Stir in quick bread mix just until dry ingredients are moistened.

3. Fill muffin cups ¼ full with batter. Drop 1 teaspoon cream cheese mixture into center of each cup. Spoon remaining batter over cream cheese mixture.

4. Sprinkle batter with remaining 2 tablespoons sugar. Bake 17 to 22 minutes or until golden brown. Cool 5 minutes. Remove from muffin cups to wire rack to cool.

Makes 12 muffins

CARROT-RAISIN BRAN MUFFINS

MAZOLA NO STICK® Cooking Spray
2 cups bran flake cereal with raisins
⅔ cup buttermilk
½ cup KARO® Dark Corn Syrup
1 cup flour
2 teaspoons baking soda
1 teaspoon ground cinnamon
¼ teaspoon salt
1 egg, slightly beaten
¼ cup sugar
¼ cup MAZOLA® Corn Oil
1 cup shredded carrots

1. Preheat oven to 400°F. Spray 12 (2½-inch) muffin pan cups with cooking spray.

2. In large bowl, mix cereal, buttermilk and corn syrup; let stand 5 minutes. In medium bowl, combine flour, baking soda, cinnamon and salt; set aside. Add egg, sugar and corn oil to cereal mixture; mix until blended. Stir in flour mixture until well blended. Stir in carrots. Spoon into prepared muffin pan cups.

3. Bake 20 minutes or until lightly browned and firm to touch. Cool in pan on wire rack 5 minutes. *Makes 12 muffins*

Cranberry Cheesecake Muffins

WHITE CHOCOLATE CHUNK MUFFINS

2½ cups all-purpose flour
1 cup packed brown sugar
⅓ cup unsweetened cocoa
    powder
2 teaspoons baking soda
½ teaspoon salt
1⅓ cups buttermilk
6 tablespoons butter, melted
2 eggs, beaten
1½ teaspoons vanilla
1½ cups chopped white
    chocolate

Preheat oven to 400°F. Grease 12 (3½-inch) large muffin cups; set aside.

Combine flour, sugar, cocoa, baking soda and salt in large bowl. Combine buttermilk, butter, eggs and vanilla in small bowl until blended. Stir into flour mixture just until moistened. Fold in white chocolate. Spoon into prepared muffin cups, filling half full.

Bake 25 to 30 minutes or until wooden pick inserted in center comes out clean. Cool in pan on wire rack 5 minutes. Remove from pan. Cool on wire rack.

Makes 12 jumbo muffins

SWEET POTATO PECAN MUFFINS

MAZOLA NO STICK®
    Cooking Spray
1¾ cups flour
⅓ cup sugar
2 teaspoons baking powder
1 teaspoon ground cinnamon
½ teaspoon salt
⅛ teaspoon ground nutmeg
¾ cup mashed cooked sweet
    potatoes
¾ cup KARO® Dark Corn
    Syrup
⅓ cup MAZOLA® Corn Oil
2 eggs
1 teaspoon vanilla
1 cup chopped pecans

1. Preheat oven to 400°F. Spray 12 (2½-inch) muffin pan cups with cooking spray.

2. In medium bowl, combine flour, sugar, baking powder, cinnamon, salt and nutmeg. In large bowl, with mixer at medium speed, beat sweet potatoes, corn syrup, corn oil, eggs and vanilla until blended. Stir into flour mixture until well blended. Stir in pecans. Spoon into prepared muffin pan cups.

3. Bake 20 minutes or until lightly browned and firm to the touch. Cool in pan on wire rack 5 minutes; remove from pan.

Makes 12 muffins

White Chocolate Chunk Muffins

HOLIDAY PUMPKIN-NUT MUFFINS

2½ cups all-purpose flour
1 cup packed light brown
    sugar
1 tablespoon baking powder
1 teaspoon ground cinnamon
½ teaspoon ground nutmeg
½ teaspoon ground ginger
¼ teaspoon salt
1 cup solid pack pumpkin
¾ cup milk
2 eggs
6 tablespoons butter, melted
⅔ cup roasted, salted pumpkin
    seeds, divided
½ cup golden raisins

Preheat oven to 400°F. Grease or paper-line 18 (2¾-inch) muffin cups.

Combine flour, brown sugar, baking powder, cinnamon, nutmeg, ginger and salt in large bowl. Stir pumpkin, milk, eggs and melted butter in medium bowl until well blended. Stir pumpkin mixture into flour mixture. Mix just until all ingredients are moistened. Stir in ⅓ cup pumpkin seeds and raisins. Spoon into prepared muffin cups, filling ⅔ full. Sprinkle remaining pumpkin seeds over muffin batter.

Bake 15 to 18 minutes or until wooden pick inserted in center comes out clean. Cool in pans 10 minutes. Remove from pans and cool completely on wire racks.

Makes 18 muffins

ORANGE COCONUT MUFFINS

¾ cup all-purpose flour
¾ cup whole wheat flour
⅔ cup toasted wheat germ
½ cup sugar
½ cup coconut
1½ teaspoons baking soda
½ teaspoon salt
1 cup sour cream
2 eggs
1 can (11 ounces) mandarin
    oranges, drained
½ cup chopped nuts

Preheat oven to 400°F. Butter 12 (2½-inch) muffin cups.

Combine flours, wheat germ, sugar, coconut, baking soda and salt in large bowl. Blend sour cream, eggs and oranges in small bowl; stir into flour mixture just until moistened. Fold in nuts. Spoon into prepared muffin cups, filling ¾ full.

Bake 18 to 20 minutes or until wooden pick inserted in center comes out clean. Remove from pan. Cool on wire rack.

Makes 12 muffins

Favorite recipe from **Wisconsin Milk Marketing Board**

Holiday Pumpkin-Nut Muffins

PECAN PEACH MUFFINS

Topping (recipe follows)
1½ cups all-purpose flour
½ cup granulated sugar
2 teaspoons baking powder
1 teaspoon ground cinnamon
¼ teaspoon salt
½ cup butter, melted
¼ cup milk
1 egg
2 medium peaches, peeled
    and diced (about 1 cup)

Preheat oven to 400°F. Grease* or paper-line 12 (2½-inch) muffin cups. Prepare Topping; set aside.

Combine flour, granulated sugar, baking powder, cinnamon and salt in large bowl. Combine butter, milk and egg in small bowl until blended; stir into flour mixture just until moistened. Fold in peaches. Spoon evenly into prepared muffin cups. Sprinkle Topping over tops of muffins.

Bake 20 to 25 minutes or until wooden pick inserted in center comes out clean. Remove from pan. *Makes 12 muffins*

Muffins can be difficult to remove from pan. For best results, use paper liners.

TOPPING:

Combine ½ cup chopped pecans, ⅓ cup packed brown sugar, ¼ cup all-purpose flour and 1 teaspoon ground cinnamon in small bowl. Add 2 tablespoons melted butter, stirring until mixture is crumbly.

Pecan Peach Muffins

Pumpkin Maple Cream Cheese Muffins

CREAM CHEESE FILLING
- 4 ounces cream cheese, softened
- 2 tablespoons packed brown sugar
- 1½ teaspoons maple flavoring

MUFFINS
- 2 cups all-purpose flour
- ¾ cup packed brown sugar
- ½ cup chopped walnuts
- 2 teaspoons baking powder
- 1 teaspoon ground cinnamon
- ½ teaspoon baking soda
- ¼ teaspoon salt
- 2 eggs
- 1 cup LIBBY'S® Solid Pack Pumpkin
- ¾ cup CARNATION® Evaporated Milk
- ¼ cup vegetable oil
- 2 teaspoons maple flavoring
  Nut topping (recipe follows)

FOR CREAM CHEESE FILLING:
COMBINE cream cheese, brown sugar and maple flavoring in small bowl until blended.

FOR MUFFINS:
COMBINE flour, brown sugar, walnuts, baking powder, cinnamon, baking soda and salt in large bowl. Combine eggs, pumpkin, evaporated milk, oil and maple flavoring; mix well. Add pumpkin mixture to flour mixture, mixing just until blended.

SPOON into 12 greased or paper-lined muffin cups (cups will be very full). Dollop 1 heaping teaspoon of Cream Cheese Filling into center of each cup, pressing into batter slightly. Sprinkle Nut Topping over muffins.

BAKE in preheated 400°F. oven for 20 to 25 minutes or until wooden pick inserted in center comes out clean. Cool in pan for 5 minutes; remove to wire rack to cool completely.

Makes 12 muffins

NUT TOPPING:
COMBINE 2 tablespoons packed brown sugar and ¼ cup chopped walnuts in small bowl.

Gingerbread Streusel Raisin Muffins

1 cup raisins
½ cup boiling water
⅓ cup margarine or butter,
    softened
¾ cup **GRANDMA'S®**
    MOLASSES
    (Unsulphured)
1 egg
2 cups all-purpose flour
1½ teaspoons baking soda
½ teaspoon salt
1 teaspoon cinnamon
1 teaspoon ginger

TOPPING
⅓ cup all-purpose flour
¼ cup firmly packed brown
    sugar
¼ cup chopped nuts
3 tablespoons margarine or
    butter
1 teaspoon cinnamon

Preheat oven to 375°F. Grease bottoms only of 12 muffin cups or line with paper baking cups. In small bowl, cover raisins with boiling water; let stand 5 minutes. In large bowl, beat ⅓ cup margarine and molasses until fluffy. Add egg; beat well. Stir in 2 cups flour, baking soda, salt, 1 teaspoon cinnamon and ginger. Blend just until dry ingredients are moistened. Gently stir in raisins and water. Fill prepared muffin cups ¾ full. For topping, combine all ingredients in small bowl. Sprinkle over muffins.

Bake 20 to 25 minutes or until toothpick inserted in centers comes out clean. Cool 5 minutes; remove from pan. Serve warm. *Makes 12 muffins*

Mocha-Macadamia Nut Muffins

MOCHA-MACADAMIA NUT MUFFINS

1¼ cups all-purpose flour
⅔ cup sugar
2½ tablespoons unsweetened
   cocoa powder
1 teaspoon baking soda
¼ teaspoon salt
⅔ cup buttermilk*
3 tablespoons butter, melted
1 egg, beaten
1 tablespoon instant coffee
   granules, dissolved in
   1 tablespoon hot water
¾ teaspoon vanilla
½ cup coarsely chopped
   macadamia nuts
Powdered sugar (optional)

*You may substitute soured fresh milk. To sour milk, place 2 teaspoons lemon juice plus enough milk to equal ⅔ cup in 2-cup measure. Stir; let stand 5 minutes before using.

PREHEAT oven to 400°F. Grease or paper-line 12 (2½-inch) muffin cups.

COMBINE flour, sugar, cocoa, baking soda and salt in large bowl. Whisk together buttermilk, butter, egg, coffee mixture and vanilla in small bowl until blended. Stir into flour mixture just until moistened. Fold in macadamia nuts. Spoon evenly into prepared muffin cups.

BAKE 13 to 17 minutes or until toothpick inserted into centers comes out clean. Cool in muffin pan on wire rack 5 minutes. Remove from pan and cool on wire rack. Sprinkle with powdered sugar, if desired. *Makes 12 muffins*

PUMPKIN-GINGER SCONES

½ cup sugar, divided
2 cups all-purpose flour
2 teaspoons baking powder
1 teaspoon ground cinnamon
½ teaspoon baking soda
½ teaspoon salt
5 tablespoons butter, divided
1 egg
½ cup solid pack pumpkin
¼ cup sour cream
½ teaspoon grated fresh
    ginger *or* 2 tablespoons
    finely chopped
    crystallized ginger

Preheat oven to 425°F.

Reserve 1 tablespoon sugar. Combine remaining sugar, flour, baking powder, cinnamon, baking soda and salt in large bowl. Cut in 4 tablespoons butter with pastry blender until mixture resembles coarse crumbs. Beat egg in small bowl. Add pumpkin, sour cream and ginger; beat until well combined. Add pumpkin mixture to flour mixture; stir until mixture forms soft dough that leaves side of bowl.

Turn dough out onto well-floured surface. Knead 10 times. Roll dough using floured rolling pin into 9×6-inch rectangle. Cut dough into 6 (3-inch) squares. Cut each square diagonally in half, making 12 triangles. Place triangles, 2 inches apart, on ungreased baking sheets. Melt remaining 1 tablespoon butter. Brush tops of triangles with butter and sprinkle with reserved sugar.

Bake 10 to 12 minutes or until golden brown. Cool 10 minutes on wire racks. *Makes 12 scones*

Pumpkin-Ginger Scones

187

QUICKY STICKY BUNS

¼ cup **KARO**® **Light or Dark Corn Syrup**
¼ cup **coarsely chopped pecans**
3 tablespoons packed brown sugar, divided
2 tablespoons softened **MAZOLA**® **Margarine, divided**
1 can (8 ounces) refrigerated crescent dinner rolls
1 teaspoon cinnamon

1. Preheat oven to 350°F.

2. In small bowl combine corn syrup, pecans, 2 tablespoons brown sugar and 1 tablespoon margarine. Spoon about 2 teaspoons mixture into each of 9 (2½-inch) muffin pan cups.

3. Unroll entire crescent roll dough; pinch seams together to form one rectangle.

4. Combine remaining 1 tablespoon brown sugar and cinnamon. Spread dough with remaining 1 tablespoon margarine; sprinkle with cinnamon mixture. Roll up from short end. Cut into 9 slices. Place one slice in each prepared cup.

5. Bake 25 minutes or until golden brown. Immediately invert pan onto cookie sheet or tray; cool.   *Makes 9 buns*

APPLE CHEDDAR SCONES

1½ cups unsifted all-purpose flour
½ cup toasted wheat germ
3 tablespoons sugar
2 teaspoons baking powder
½ teaspoon salt
2 tablespoons butter
1 small Washington Rome apple, cored and chopped
¼ cup shredded Cheddar cheese
1 large egg white
½ cup low-fat (1%) milk

1. Heat oven to 400°F. Grease an 8-inch round cake pan. In medium bowl, combine flour, wheat germ, sugar, baking powder and salt. With pastry blender, cut in butter until the size of coarse crumbs. Toss apple and cheese in flour mixture.

2. Beat together egg white and milk until well combined. Add to flour mixture, mixing with fork until dough forms. Turn dough out onto lightly floured surface and knead 6 times.

3. Spread dough evenly in cake pan and score deeply with knife into 6 wedges. Bake 25 to 30 minutes or until top springs back when gently pressed. Let stand 5 minutes; remove from pan. Cool completely.   *Makes 6 scones*

Favorite recipe from **Washington Apple Commission**

Quicky Sticky Buns

189

FRUITED OAT SCONES

1½ cups all-purpose flour
1¼ cups QUAKER® Oats (quick
    or old fashioned,
    uncooked)
¼ cup sugar
1 tablespoon baking powder
¼ teaspoon salt (optional)
⅓ cup (5⅓ tablespoons)
    margarine
1 (6-ounce) package
    (1⅓ cups) diced dried
    mixed fruit
½ cup milk
1 egg, slightly beaten
1 teaspoon sugar
⅛ teaspoon ground cinnamon

Preheat oven to 375°F. Combine flour, oats, ¼ cup sugar, baking powder and salt; mix well. Cut in margarine until mixture resembles coarse crumbs; stir in fruit. Add milk and egg, mixing just until moistened. Shape dough to form a ball. Turn out onto floured surface; knead gently 6 times. On lightly greased cookie sheet, pat out dough to form 8-inch circle. With sharp knife, score round into 12 wedges; sprinkle with combined 1 teaspoon sugar and cinnamon. Bake about 30 minutes or until golden brown. Break apart; serve warm.

Makes 1 dozen scones

Fruited Oat Scones

CRANBERRY SCONES

2½ cups all-purpose flour
½ cup packed brown sugar
1 tablespoon baking powder
1 teaspoon baking soda
¾ teaspoon salt
½ teaspoon ground cinnamon
¼ cup Prune Purée (recipe follows) or prepared prune butter
2 tablespoons cold margarine or butter
1 container (8 ounces) nonfat vanilla yogurt
¾ cup dried cranberries
1 egg white, lightly beaten
1 tablespoon granulated sugar

Preheat oven to 400°F. Coat baking sheet with vegetable cooking spray. In large bowl, combine flour, brown sugar, baking powder, baking soda, salt and cinnamon. Cut in Prune Purée and margarine with pastry blender until mixture resembles coarse crumbs. Mix in yogurt just until blended. Stir in cranberries. On floured surface, roll or pat dough to ¾-inch thickness. Cut out with 2½- to 3-inch biscuit cutter, rerolling scraps as needed, but handling as little as possible. Arrange on prepared baking sheet, spacing 2 inches apart. Brush with egg white and sprinkle with granulated sugar. Bake in center of oven about 15 minutes until golden brown and springy to the touch. Serve warm or at room temperature.

Makes 12 scones

PRUNE PURÉE:

Combine 1⅓ cups (8 ounces) pitted prunes and 6 tablespoons hot water in container of food processor or blender. Pulse on and off until prunes are finely chopped and smooth. Store leftovers in a covered container in the refrigerator for up to two months. Makes 1 cup.

Favorite recipe from **California Prune Board**

Cranberry Scones

193

Pear Scones

1 pear, cored
2½ cups all-purpose flour
1 cup granulated sugar
½ cup whole wheat flour
1 tablespoon baking powder
½ teaspoon baking soda
½ teaspoon ground ginger
2 tablespoons cold margarine
2 tablespoons cold butter
½ cup buttermilk
1 tablespoon granulated
    sugar

Preheat oven to 400°F. Spray baking sheets with nonstick cooking spray; set aside.

In food processor shred pear. Remove from work bowl; set aside. In food processor combine all-purpose flour, 1 cup sugar, whole wheat flour, baking powder, baking soda and ginger; process until blended. Add margarine and butter; process until mixture resembles coarse crumbs. Transfer to large bowl. Stir in reserved pear and buttermilk until soft dough forms.

Turn out dough onto lightly floured surface. Knead 8 to 10 times. Roll out dough into ½-inch thickness; cut into rounds with lightly floured 2½-inch biscuit cutter. Sprinkle 1 tablespoon sugar over tops of scones.

Bake 10 to 15 minutes or until golden brown and wooden pick inserted in center comes out clean. Remove from baking sheets. Cool on wire racks.   *Makes about 30 scones*

Favorite recipe from **The Sugar Association, Inc.**

PEACH-ALMOND SCONES

2 cups all-purpose flour
¼ cup plus 1 tablespoon
    sugar, divided
2 teaspoons baking powder
½ teaspoon salt
5 tablespoons butter
½ cup sliced almonds, lightly
    toasted, divided
2 tablespoons milk
1 egg
1 can (16 ounces) peaches,
    drained and finely
    chopped
½ teaspoon almond extract

PREHEAT oven to 425°F. Combine flour, ¼ cup sugar, baking powder and salt in large bowl. Cut in butter with pastry blender or 2 knives until mixture resembles coarse crumbs. Stir in ¼ cup almonds. Lightly beat milk and egg in small bowl. Reserve 2 tablespoons milk mixture; set aside. Stir peaches and almond extract into remaining milk mixture. Stir into flour mixture until soft dough forms.

TURN out dough onto well-floured surface. Gently knead 10 to 12 times. Roll out into 9×6-inch rectangle. Cut dough into 6 (3-inch) squares using floured knife; cut diagonally into halves, forming 12 triangles. Place 2 inches apart on ungreased baking sheets. Brush triangles with reserved milk mixture. Sprinkle with remaining ¼ cup almonds and 1 tablespoon sugar.

BAKE 10 to 12 minutes or until golden brown. Remove from baking sheets and cool on wire racks 10 minutes. Serve warm. *Makes 12 scones*

COOKIE TIN EXPRESS

JOLLY PEANUT BUTTER GINGERBREAD COOKIES

1⅔ cups (10-ounce package) REESE'S® Peanut Butter Chips
¾ cup (1½ sticks) butter or margarine, softened
1 cup packed light brown sugar
1 cup dark corn syrup
2 eggs
5 cups all-purpose flour
1 teaspoon baking soda
½ teaspoon ground cinnamon
¼ teaspoon ground ginger
¼ teaspoon salt

1. In small microwave-safe bowl, place peanut butter chips. Microwave at HIGH (100%) 1 to 2 minutes or until chips are melted when stirred. In large bowl, beat melted peanut butter chips and butter until well blended. Add brown sugar, corn syrup and eggs; beat until light and fluffy. Stir together flour, baking soda, cinnamon, ginger and salt. Add half of flour mixture to butter mixture; beat on low speed of electric mixer until smooth. With wooden spoon, stir in remaining flour mixture until well blended. Divide into thirds; wrap each in plastic wrap. Refrigerate at least 1 hour or until dough is firm enough to roll.

2. Heat oven to 325°F.

3. On lightly floured surface, roll 1 dough portion at a time to ⅛-inch thickness; with floured cookie cutters, cut into holiday shapes. Place on ungreased cookie sheet.

4. Bake 10 to 12 minutes or until set and lightly browned. Cool slightly; remove from cookie sheet to wire rack. Cool completely. Frost and decorate as desired.

Makes about 6 dozen cookies

Jolly Peanut Butter Gingerbread Cookies

BUTTERY ALMOND CUTOUTS

1½ cups granulated sugar
1 cup butter, softened
¾ cup sour cream
2 eggs
3 teaspoons almond extract, divided
1 teaspoon vanilla
4⅓ cups all-purpose flour
1 teaspoon baking powder
1 teaspoon baking soda
½ teaspoon salt
2 cups powdered sugar
2 tablespoons milk
1 tablespoon light corn syrup
Food color

1. Beat sugar and butter in large bowl until light and fluffy. Add sour cream, eggs, 2 teaspoons almond extract and vanilla; beat until smooth. Add flour, baking powder, baking soda and salt; beat just until well blended.

2. Divide dough into 4 pieces; flatten each piece into disk. Wrap each disk tightly with plastic wrap. Refrigerate at least 3 hours or up to 3 days.

3. Preheat oven to 375°F. Working with 1 disk of dough at a time, roll dough out onto floured surface to ¼-inch thickness. Cut dough into desired shapes using 2½-inch cookie cutters. Place about 2 inches apart onto ungreased baking sheets. Bake 7 to 8 minutes or until edges are firm and bottoms are brown. Remove from baking sheets to wire rack to cool.

4. Combine powdered sugar, milk, corn syrup and remaining 1 teaspoon almond extract in small bowl; stir until smooth.

5. Divide icing among 3 or 4 small bowls; tint with desired food color. Frost cookies.   *Makes about 3 dozen cookies*

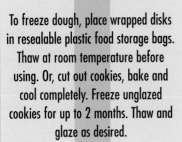

To freeze dough, place wrapped disks in resealable plastic food storage bags. Thaw at room temperature before using. Or, cut out cookies, bake and cool completely. Freeze unglazed cookies for up to 2 months. Thaw and glaze as desired.

Buttery Almond Cutouts

Holiday Wreath Cookies

1 package (20 ounces)
    refrigerated sugar cookie
    dough
2 cups shredded coconut
2 to 3 drops green food color
1 container (16 ounces)
    ready-to-spread French
    vanilla frosting
    Green sugar or small
    cinnamon candies

1. Preheat oven to 350°F. Divide cookie dough in half (keep half of dough refrigerated until needed). Roll dough out on well-floured surface to ⅛-inch-thick rectangle. Cut with cookie cutters to resemble wreaths. Repeat with remaining dough.

2. Place cookies about 2 inches apart onto ungreased baking sheets. Bake 7 to 9 minutes or until edges are lightly browned. Remove cookies from baking sheets to wire rack to cool completely.

3. Place coconut in plastic food storage bag. Add food color; seal bag and shake until coconut is evenly colored. Frost cookies with frosting and decorate with coconut or green sugar and cinnamon candies.

Makes about 2 dozen cookies

Lemony Butter Cookies

½ cup butter, softened
½ cup sugar
1 egg
1½ cups all-purpose flour
1 teaspoon grated lemon peel
2 tablespoons fresh lemon
    juice
½ teaspoon baking powder
⅛ teaspoon salt
    Additional sugar

Beat butter and sugar in large bowl with electric mixer until creamy. Beat in egg until light and fluffy. Mix in flour, lemon peel and juice, baking powder and salt. Cover; refrigerate about 2 hours or until firm.

Preheat oven to 350°F. Roll out dough, a small portion at a time, on well-floured surface to ¼-inch thickness. (Keep remaining dough in refrigerator.) Cut with 3-inch round cookie cutter. Transfer to ungreased cookie sheets. Repeat with remaining dough. Sprinkle with sugar.

Bake 8 to 10 minutes or until lightly browned on edges. Cool 1 minute on cookie sheets. Remove to wire racks; cool completely. Store in airtight container.

Makes about 2½ dozen cookies

Holiday Wreath Cookies

Chocolate Reindeer

1 cup butter, softened
1 cup sugar
1 egg
1 teaspoon vanilla
2 ounces semisweet
    chocolate, melted
2¼ cups all-purpose flour
1 teaspoon baking powder
¼ teaspoon salt
    Royal Icing (recipe follows)
    Assorted small candies

1. Beat butter and sugar in large bowl with electric mixer at high speed until fluffy. Beat in egg and vanilla. Add melted chocolate; mix well. Add flour, baking powder and salt; mix well. Cover and refrigerate about 2 hours or until firm.

2. Preheat oven to 325°F. Grease 2 cookie sheets; set aside.

3. Divide dough in half. Reserve 1 half; wrap remaining dough in plastic wrap and refrigerate.

4. Roll reserved dough on well-floured surface to ¼-inch thickness. Cut with reindeer cookie cutter. Place 2 inches apart on prepared cookie sheet. Chill 10 minutes.

5. Bake 13 to 15 minutes or until set. Cool completely on cookie sheets. Repeat steps with remaining dough.

6. Prepare Royal Icing.

7. To decorate, pipe assorted colored icing on reindeer and add small candies. Let cookies dry uncovered before storing in airtight container at room temperature.

Makes 16 (4-inch) reindeer

Royal Icing

2 to 3 large egg whites
2 to 4 cups powdered sugar
1 tablespoon lemon juice

Beat 2 egg whites in medium bowl with electric mixer until peaks just begin to hold their shape. Add 2 cups sugar and lemon juice; beat for 1 minute. If consistency is too thin for piping, gradually add more sugar until desired result is achieved; if it is too thick, add another egg white. Divide icing among several small bowls and tint to desired colors.

RASPBERRY LINZER ROUNDS

1¼ cups granulated sugar
1 Butter Flavor* CRISCO®
    Stick or 1 cup Butter
    Flavor* CRISCO® all-
    vegetable shortening
2 eggs
¼ cup light corn syrup or
    regular pancake syrup
1 teaspoon vanilla
1 teaspoon almond extract
3 cups all-purpose flour (plus
    4 tablespoons), divided
1 cup ground almonds (about
    4 to 5 ounces)
¾ teaspoon baking powder
½ teaspoon baking soda
½ teaspoon salt
½ cup seedless raspberry
    preserves, stirred
Confectioners' sugar

Butter Flavor Crisco is artificially flavored.

1. Place granulated sugar and shortening in large bowl. Beat at medium speed of electric mixer until well blended. Add eggs, syrup, vanilla and almond extract; beat until blended and fluffy.

2. Combine 3 cups flour, ground almonds, baking powder, baking soda and salt. Add gradually to shortening mixture, beating at low speed until well blended.

3. Divide dough into 4 pieces; shape each piece into disk. Wrap with plastic wrap. Refrigerate several hours or until firm.

4. Heat oven to 375°F. Place sheets of foil on countertop for cooling cookies.

5. Sprinkle about 1 tablespoon flour on large sheet of waxed paper. Place disk of dough on floured paper; flatten slightly with hands. Turn dough over and cover with another large sheet of waxed paper. Roll dough to ¼-inch thickness. Remove top sheet of waxed paper. Cut out with 2- or 2½-inch floured scalloped round cookie cutter. Place 2 inches apart on ungreased baking sheet. Repeat with remaining dough. Cut out centers of half the cookies with ½- or ¾-inch round cookie cutter.

6. Bake one baking sheet at a time at 375°F for 5 to 7 minutes or until edges of cookies are lightly browned. *Do not overbake.* Cool 2 minutes on baking sheet. Remove cookies to foil to cool completely.

7. Spread a small amount of raspberry jam on bottom of solid cookies; cover with cut-out cookies, bottom sides down, to form sandwiches. Sift confectioners' sugar, if desired, over tops of cookies.   *Makes about 2 dozen cookies*

Christmas Cookie Pops

CHRISTMAS COOKIE POPS

1 package (20 ounces) refrigerated sugar cookie dough
All-purpose flour
20 to 24 (4-inch) lollipop sticks
Royal Icing (page 202)
6 ounces almond bark, (vanilla or chocolate), or butterscotch chips
Vegetable shortening
Assorted small candies

1. Preheat oven to 350°F. Grease cookie sheets; set aside.

2. Divide cookie dough in half. (Keep half of dough refrigerated until needed.)

3. Roll dough out on well-floured surface to ⅓-inch thickness. Cut out cookies using 3¼- or 3½-inch Christmas cookie cutters. Place lollipop sticks on cookies so that tips of sticks are embedded in cookies. Carefully turn cookies with spatula so sticks are in back; place on prepared cookie sheets. Repeat with remaining half of dough.

4. Bake 7 to 11 minutes or until edges are lightly browned. Cool cookies on sheets 2 minutes. Remove cookies to wire racks; cool completely.

5. Prepare Royal Icing.

6. Melt almond bark in medium microwavable bowl according to package directions. Add 1 or more tablespoons shortening if coating is too thick. Hold cookies over bowl; spoon coating over cookies. Scrape excess coating from cookie edges. Decorate with small candies and Royal Icing immediately. Place cookies on wire racks set over waxed paper; let harden. Store in tin at room temperature.

Makes 20 to 24 cookies

GINGERBREAD PEOPLE

½ cup butter, softened
½ cup packed brown sugar
⅓ cup molasses
⅓ cup water
1 egg
4 cups all-purpose flour
2 teaspoons baking soda
1 teaspoon ground ginger
½ teaspoon ground allspice
½ teaspoon ground cinnamon
½ teaspoon ground cloves
   White or colored decorators
      frostings

Beat butter and brown sugar in large bowl with electric mixer until creamy. Add molasses, water and egg; beat until blended. Stir in flour, baking soda, ginger, allspice, cinnamon and cloves until well blended. Cover; refrigerate about 2 hours or until firm.

Preheat oven to 350°F. Grease cookie sheets. Roll out dough to ⅛-inch thickness on lightly floured surface with lightly floured rolling pin. Cut with cookie cutter. Place 2 inches apart on prepared cookie sheets.

Bake 12 to 15 minutes until firm to the touch. Cool 1 minute on cookie sheets. Remove to wire racks; cool completely. Decorate with frostings. Store in airtight containers.

Makes about 4½ dozen cookies

FESTIVE LEBKUCHEN

3 tablespoons butter
1 cup packed brown sugar
¼ cup honey
1 egg
   Grated peel and juice of
      1 lemon
3 cups all-purpose flour
2 teaspoons ground allspice
½ teaspoon baking soda
½ teaspoon salt
   White decorators frosting

Melt butter with brown sugar and honey in medium saucepan over low heat, stirring constantly. Pour into large bowl. Cool 30 minutes. Add egg, lemon peel and juice; beat 2 minutes with electric mixer on high speed. Stir in flour, allspice, baking soda and salt until well blended. Cover; refrigerate overnight or up to 3 days.

Preheat oven to 350°F. Grease cookie sheet. Roll out dough to ½-inch thickness on lightly floured surface with lightly floured rolling pin. Cut with 3-inch cookie cutter. Transfer to prepared cookie sheet. Bake 15 to 18 minutes until edges are light brown. Cool 1 minute. Remove to wire rack; cool completely. Decorate with white frosting. Store in airtight container.

Makes 1 dozen cookies

Gingerbread People

ELEPHANT EARS

1 package (17¼ ounces) frozen puff pastry, thawed according to package directions
1 egg, beaten
¼ cup sugar, divided
2 squares (1 ounce each) semisweet chocolate

Preheat oven to 375°F. Grease cookie sheets; sprinkle lightly with water. Roll one sheet of pastry to 12×10-inch rectangle. Brush with egg; sprinkle with 1 tablespoon sugar. Tightly roll up 10-inch sides, meeting in center. Brush center with egg and seal rolls tightly together; turn over. Cut into ⅜-inch-thick slices. Place slices on prepared cookie sheets. Sprinkle with 1 tablespoon sugar. Repeat with remaining pastry, egg and sugar. Bake 16 to 18 minutes until golden brown. Remove to wire racks; cool completely.

Melt chocolate in small saucepan over low heat, stirring constantly. Remove from heat. Spread bottoms of cookies with chocolate. Place on wire rack, chocolate side up. Let stand until chocolate is set. Store between layers of waxed paper in airtight containers. *Makes about 4 dozen cookies*

GOLDEN KOLACKY

½ cup butter, softened
4 ounces cream cheese, softened
1 cup flour
Fruit preserves

Combine butter and cream cheese in large bowl; beat until smooth and creamy. Gradually add flour to butter mixture, blending until mixture forms soft dough. Divide dough in half; wrap each half in plastic wrap. Refrigerate until firm.

Preheat oven to 375°F. Roll out dough, ½ at a time, on floured surface to ⅛-inch thickness. Cut into 3-inch squares. Spoon 1 teaspoon preserves in center of each square. Bring up two opposite corners to center; pinch together tightly to seal. Fold sealed tip to one side; pinch to seal. Place 1 inch apart on ungreased cookie sheets. Bake for 10 to 15 minutes or until lightly browned. Remove to cooling racks; cool completely. *Makes about 2½ dozen cookies*

Top to bottom: Elephant Ears and Chocolate Raspberry Thumbprints (page 244)

MINCEMEAT PASTRIES

3½ cups all-purpose flour
¾ cup granulated sugar
½ teaspoon salt
½ cup (1 stick) butter, chilled
8 tablespoons vegetable
    shortening
1 cup buttermilk
1 cup mincemeat
¼ cup powdered sugar
    (optional)

1. Combine flour, granulated sugar and salt in large bowl; set aside.

2. Cut butter into 1-inch chunks. Add butter and shortening to flour mixture. Cut in with pastry blender or 2 knives until mixture resembles coarse crumbs. Drizzle buttermilk over top; toss just until mixture comes together into a ball.

3. Turn out dough onto lightly floured work surface; fold in half and flatten to about ½ inch thick. Knead about eight times. Divide dough in half; press each half into ½-inch-thick disk. Wrap in plastic wrap and refrigerate at least 30 minutes.

4. Preheat oven to 350°F. Lightly grease cookie sheets; set aside. Let dough rest at room temperature 10 minutes. Roll one disk of dough into 18×12-inch rectangle on lightly floured work surface. Cut into 24 (3-inch) squares. Place heaping ½ teaspoon mincemeat in center of each square. Fold one corner about ⅔ of the way over the filling; fold opposite corner ⅔ of the way over the filling.

5. Place 2 inches apart on prepared cookie sheets. Repeat with remaining dough.

6. Bake 20 minutes or until lightly browned. Remove cookies to wire rack; cool completely. Sprinkle tops of pastries lightly with powdered sugar.   *Makes 4 dozen cookies*

Mincemeat Pastries

Chocolate Biscotti Nuggets

¾ cup old-fashioned or quick oats

2¼ cups all-purpose flour

1½ teaspoons baking powder

½ teaspoon salt

¾ cup chopped dates

½ cup coarsely chopped toasted pecans

½ cup honey

2 large eggs

1 teaspoon vanilla

½ cup butter, melted

Grated peel of 2 oranges

CHOCOLATE COATING

1¾ cups semisweet dark chocolate or white chocolate chips

4 teaspoons shortening

1. Grease baking sheet; set aside. Preheat oven to 350°F.

2. Place oats in food processor; process until oats resemble coarse flour. Combine oats, flour, baking powder and salt in large bowl. Stir in dates and pecans. Set aside.

3. Whisk together honey, eggs and vanilla in medium bowl. Add melted butter and orange peel. Stir egg mixture into oat mixture just until blended. Turn out dough onto lightly floured surface; flatten slightly. Knead until dough holds together, adding flour if necessary to prevent sticking. Divide dough into 3 equal pieces; roll each into 9×½-inch log. Carefully transfer logs to prepared baking sheet, spacing about 2 inches apart. If dough cracks, pat back into shape.

4. Bake logs 25 to 30 minutes or until lightly golden but still soft. Remove from oven. Reduce oven temperature to 275°F. Let logs cool on baking sheet 10 minutes. Trim ends using serrated knife. Slice logs on slight diagonal about ¾ inch thick. Arrange biscotti on their sides on baking sheet. Return to oven and bake 15 to 20 minutes or until lightly golden. Turn biscotti over and bake 10 to 15 minutes longer. Remove biscotti to wire rack to cool completely.

5. Brush individual biscotti with dry pastry brush to remove any loose crumbs. Heat chocolate chips and shortening in small heavy saucepan over very low heat until melted and smooth. Dip half of each biscotti slice into melted chocolate, letting any excess run off. Place on prepared baking sheet. Let stand until set. Store between layers of waxed paper in airtight container.   *Makes about 36 biscotti slices*

Chocolate Biscotti Nuggets

Slice 'n' Bake Ginger Wafers

1 cup packed brown sugar
½ cup butter, softened
¼ cup light molasses
1 egg
2 teaspoons ground ginger
1 teaspoon grated orange peel
¼ teaspoon salt
¼ teaspoon ground cinnamon
¼ teaspoon ground cloves
2 cups all-purpose flour

1. Beat sugar, butter and molasses in large bowl until light and fluffy. Add egg, ginger, orange peel, salt, cinnamon and cloves; beat until well blended. Stir in flour until well blended. (Dough will be very stiff.)

2. Divide dough in half. Roll each half into 8×1½-inch log. Wrap logs in wax paper or plastic wrap; refrigerate at least 5 hours or up to 5 days.

3. Preheat oven to 350°F. Cut dough into ¼-inch-thick slices. Place about 2 inches apart onto ungreased baking sheets. Bake 12 to 14 minutes or until set. Remove from baking sheet to wire rack to cool. *Makes about 4½ dozen cookies*

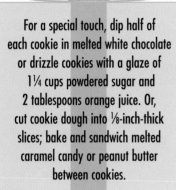

For a special touch, dip half of each cookie in melted white chocolate or drizzle cookies with a glaze of 1¼ cups powdered sugar and 2 tablespoons orange juice. Or, cut cookie dough into ⅛-inch-thick slices; bake and sandwich melted caramel candy or peanut butter between cookies.

Slice 'n' Bake Ginger Wafers

Choco-Coco Pecan Crisps

1 cup packed light brown sugar
½ cup butter, softened
1 egg
1 teaspoon vanilla
1½ cups all-purpose flour
1 cup chopped pecans
⅓ cup unsweetened cocoa
½ teaspoon baking soda
1 cup flaked coconut

Cream sugar and butter in large bowl until light and fluffy. Beat in egg and vanilla. Combine flour, pecans, cocoa and baking soda in small bowl until well blended. Add to creamed mixture, blending until stiff dough is formed. Sprinkle coconut on work surface. Divide dough into 4 parts. Shape each part into a roll about 1½ inches in diameter; roll in coconut until thickly coated. Wrap in plastic wrap; refrigerate until firm, at least 1 hour or up to 2 weeks. (For longer storage, freeze up to 6 weeks.)

Preheat oven to 350°F. Cut rolls into ⅛-inch-thick slices. Place 2 inches apart on ungreased cookie sheets. Bake 10 to 13 minutes or until firm, but not overly browned. Remove to wire racks to cool. *Makes about 6 dozen cookies*

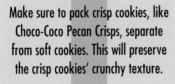

Make sure to pack crisp cookies, like Choco-Coco Pecan Crisps, separate from soft cookies. This will preserve the crisp cookies' crunchy texture.

Left to right: Choco-Coco Pecan Crisps and Holiday Fruit Drops (page 246)

ORANGE-CARDAMOM THINS

1¼ cups granulated sugar
1 Butter Flavor* CRISCO®
    Stick or 1 cup Butter
    Flavor* CRISCO® all-
    vegetable shortening
1 egg
¼ cup light corn syrup or
    regular pancake syrup
1 teaspoon vanilla
1 tablespoon grated orange
    peel
½ teaspoon orange extract
3 cups all-purpose flour
1¼ teaspoons cardamom
¾ teaspoon baking powder
½ teaspoon baking soda
½ teaspoon salt
½ teaspoon cinnamon

*Butter Flavor Crisco is artificially flavored.

1. Place sugar and shortening in large bowl. Beat at medium speed of electric mixer until well blended. Add egg, syrup, vanilla, orange peel and orange extract; beat until well blended and fluffy.

2. Combine flour, cardamom, baking powder, baking soda, salt and cinnamon. Add gradually to shortening mixture, beating at low speed until well blended.

3. Divide dough in half. Roll each half into 12-inch-long log. Wrap with plastic wrap. Refrigerate for 4 hours or until firm.

4. Heat oven to 375°F. Grease baking sheets. Place sheets of foil on counter for cooling cookies.

5. Cut rolls into ¼-inch-thick slices. Place 1 inch apart on prepared baking sheets.

6. Bake one baking sheet at a time at 375°F for 7 to 9 minutes or until bottoms of cookies are lightly browned. *Do not overbake.* Cool 2 minutes on baking sheet. Remove cookies to foil to cool completely.

Makes about 5 dozen cookies

Cocoa Pecan Crescents

1 cup (2 sticks) butter or margarine, softened
⅔ cup granulated sugar
1½ teaspoons vanilla extract
1¾ cups all-purpose flour
⅓ cup HERSHEY'S Cocoa
⅛ teaspoon salt
1½ cups ground pecans
Powdered sugar

In large mixer bowl, beat butter, granulated sugar and vanilla until light and fluffy. Stir together flour, cocoa and salt. Add to butter mixture; blend well. Stir in pecans. Refrigerate dough 1 hour or until firm enough to handle. Heat oven to 375°F. Shape scant 1 tablespoon dough into log about 2½ inches long; place on ungreased cookie sheet. Shape each log into crescent, tapering ends. Bake 13 to 15 minutes or until set. Cool slightly; remove from cookie sheet to wire rack. Cool completely. Roll in powdered sugar.

Makes about 3½ dozen cookies

Almond Crescents

1 cup butter, softened
⅓ cup sugar
1¾ cups all-purpose flour
¼ cup cornstarch
1 teaspoon vanilla extract
1½ cups ground almonds, toasted*
Chocolate Glaze (recipe follows) or powdered sugar

To toast almonds, spread on cookie sheet. Bake at 325°F for 4 minutes or until fragrant and golden.

Preheat oven to 325°F. Beat butter and sugar in large bowl until fluffy. Mix in flour, cornstarch and vanilla. Stir in almonds. Shape tablespoonfuls of dough into crescents. Place 2 inches apart on ungreased cookie sheets. Bake 22 to 25 minutes or until light brown. Cool 1 minute. Remove to wire racks; cool completely. Drizzle with Chocolate Glaze, if desired. Allow chocolate to set, then store in airtight container. Or, before serving, sprinkle with powdered sugar.

Makes about 3 dozen cookies

Chocolate Glaze:

Place ½ cup semisweet chocolate chips and 1 tablespoon butter or margarine in small resealable plastic bag. Place bag in bowl of hot water for 2 to 3 minutes or until chocolate is softened. Dry with paper towel. Knead until chocolate mixture is smooth. Cut off very tiny corner of bag. Drizzle chocolate mixture over cookies.

219

Chocolate-Dipped Orange Logs

CHOCOLATE-DIPPED ORANGE LOGS

3¼ cups all-purpose flour
⅓ teaspoon salt
1 cup butter, softened
1 cup sugar
2 eggs
1½ teaspoons grated orange
   peel
1 teaspoon vanilla
1 package (12 ounces)
   semisweet chocolate
   chips
1½ cups pecan pieces, finely
   chopped

COMBINE flour and salt in medium bowl. Beat butter in large bowl with electric mixer at medium speed until smooth. Gradually beat in sugar; increase speed to high and beat until light and fluffy. Beat in eggs, 1 at a time, blending well after each addition. Beat in orange peel and vanilla until blended. Gradually stir in flour mixture until blended. (Dough will be crumbly.)

GATHER dough together and press gently to form a ball. Flatten into disk; wrap in plastic wrap and refrigerate 2 hours or until firm. (Dough can be prepared one day in advance and refrigerated overnight.)

PREHEAT oven to 350°F. Shape dough into 1-inch balls. Roll balls on flat surface with fingertips to form 3-inch logs about ½ inch thick. Place logs 1 inch apart on greased cookie sheets.

BAKE 16 to 18 minutes or until bottoms of cookies are golden brown. (Cookies will feel soft and look white on top; they will become crisp when cool.) Transfer to wire racks to cool completely.

MELT chocolate chips in medium heavy saucepan over low heat. Place chopped pecans on sheet of waxed paper. Dip one end of each cookie in chocolate, shaking off excess. Roll chocolate-covered ends in pecans. Place on waxed paper-lined cookie sheets and let stand until chocolate is set, or refrigerate about 5 minutes to set chocolate. Store in airtight container. *Makes about 36 cookies*

Snowmen

1 package (20 ounces)
  refrigerated chocolate
  chip cookie dough
1½ cups sifted powdered sugar
2 tablespoons milk
  Candy corn, gum drops,
  chocolate chips, licorice
  and other assorted small
  candies

These easy-to-make cookies are the perfect project for children. Provide a variety of candy and watch their imaginations run wild decorating their own unique snowpeople.

1. Preheat oven to 375°F.

2. Cut dough into 12 equal sections. Divide each section into 3 balls: large, medium and small for each snowman.

3. For each snowman, place 3 balls in a row, ¼ inch apart, on ungreased cookie sheet. Repeat with remaining dough.

4. Bake 10 to 12 minutes or until edges are very lightly browned.

5. Cool 4 minutes on cookie sheets. Remove to wire racks; cool completely.

6. Mix powdered sugar and milk in medium bowl until smooth. Pour over cookies. Let cookies stand 20 minutes or until set.

7. Decorate to create faces, hats and arms with assorted candies.   *Makes 1 dozen cookies*

Snowmen

HONEY SPICE BALLS

½ cup butter, softened
½ cup packed brown sugar
1 egg
1 tablespoon honey
1 teaspoon vanilla extract
2 cups all-purpose flour
½ teaspoon baking powder
½ teaspoon ground cinnamon
¼ teaspoon ground nutmeg
   Uncooked quick oats

Preheat oven to 350°F. Grease cookie sheets. Beat butter and brown sugar in large bowl with electric mixer until creamy. Add egg, honey and vanilla; beat until light and fluffy. Stir in flour, baking powder, cinnamon and nutmeg until well blended. Shape tablespoonfuls of dough into balls; roll in oats. Place 2 inches apart on prepared cookie sheets.

Bake 15 to 18 minutes until cookie tops crack slightly. Cool 1 minute on cookie sheets. Remove to wire racks; cool completely. Store in airtight container.

Makes about 2½ dozen cookies

HOMEMADE COCONUT MACAROONS

3 egg whites
¼ teaspoon cream of tartar
⅛ teaspoon salt
¾ cup sugar
2¼ cups shredded coconut, toasted*
1 teaspoon vanilla extract

To toast coconut, spread evenly on cookie sheet. Toast in 350°F oven for 3 minutes. Stir and toast 1 to 2 minutes more until light golden brown.

Preheat oven to 325°F. Line cookie sheets with parchment paper or foil. Beat egg whites, cream of tartar and salt in large bowl with electric mixer until soft peaks form. Beat in sugar, 1 tablespoon at a time, until egg whites are stiff and shiny. Fold in coconut and vanilla. Drop tablespoonfuls of dough 4 inches apart onto prepared cookie sheets; spread each into 3-inch circles with back of spoon.

Bake 18 to 22 minutes until light brown. Cool 1 minute on cookie sheets. Remove to wire racks; cool completely. Store in airtight container.

Makes about 2 dozen cookies

Left to right: Homemade Coconut Macaroons and Honey Spice Balls

MOLASSES SPICE COOKIES

1 cup granulated sugar
¾ cup shortening
¼ cup molasses
1 large egg, beaten
2 cups all-purpose flour
2 teaspoons baking soda
1 teaspoon ground cinnamon
1 teaspoon ground cloves
1 teaspoon ground ginger
¼ teaspoon dry mustard
¼ teaspoon salt
½ cup granulated brown sugar

1. Preheat oven to 375°F. Grease cookie sheets; set aside.

2. Beat granulated sugar and shortening about 5 minutes in large bowl until light and fluffy. Add molasses and egg; beat until fluffy.

3. Combine flour, baking soda, cinnamon, cloves, ginger, mustard and salt in medium bowl. Add to shortening mixture; mix until just combined.

4. Place brown sugar in shallow dish. Roll tablespoonfuls of dough into 1-inch balls; roll in sugar to coat. Place 2 inches apart on prepared cookie sheets. Bake 15 minutes or until lightly browned. Let cookies stand on cookie sheets 2 minutes. Remove cookies to wire racks; cool completely.

Makes about 6 dozen cookies

Looking for something different to take to all your holiday gatherings? Decorate a metal tin with rubber stamps for a crafty look and fill it with Molasses Spice Cookies and an assortment of uniquely flavored teas.

Molasses Spice Cookies

WALNUT CHRISTMAS BALLS

1 cup California walnuts
⅔ cup powdered sugar, divided
1 cup butter or margarine, softened
1 teaspoon vanilla
1¾ cups all-purpose flour
Chocolate Filling (recipe follows)

In food processor or blender, process walnuts with 2 tablespoons of the sugar until finely ground; set aside. In large bowl, cream butter and remaining sugar. Beat in vanilla. Add flour and ¾ cup of the walnuts; mix until blended. Roll dough into about 3 dozen walnut-size balls. Place 2 inches apart on ungreased cookie sheets. Bake in preheated 350°F oven 10 to 12 minutes or until just golden around edges. Remove to wire racks to cool completely. Prepare Chocolate Filling. Place generous teaspoonful of filling on flat side of half the cookies. Top with remaining cookies, flat side down, forming sandwiches. Roll chocolate edges of cookies in remaining ground walnuts.

Makes about 1½ dozen sandwich cookies

CHOCOLATE FILLING:

Chop 3 squares (1 ounce each) semisweet chocolate into small pieces; place in food processor or blender with ½ teaspoon vanilla. In small saucepan, heat 2 tablespoons each butter or margarine and whipping cream over medium heat until hot; pour over chocolate. Process until chocolate is melted, turning machine off and scraping sides as needed. With machine running, gradually add 1 cup powdered sugar; process until smooth.

Favorite recipe from the **Walnut Marketing Board**

CHOCOLATE-DIPPED ALMOND HORNS

1½ cups powdered sugar
1 cup butter, softened
2 egg yolks
1½ teaspoons vanilla
2 cups all-purpose flour
½ cup ground almonds
1 teaspoon cream of tartar
1 teaspoon baking soda
1 cup semisweet chocolate
    chips, melted
   Powdered sugar

1. Preheat oven to 325°F. Beat sugar and butter in large bowl with electric mixer at medium speed until fluffy, about 1 to 2 minutes.

2. Add egg yolks and vanilla; continue beating until well blended, 1 to 2 minutes.

3. Reduce speed to low. Add flour, almonds, cream of tartar and baking soda. Continue beating, scraping bowl often, until well mixed, 1 to 2 minutes.

4. Shape into 1-inch balls. Roll balls into 2½-inch ropes; shape into crescents. Place crescents 2 inches apart on greased cookie sheets. Flatten slightly with glass bottom covered in waxed paper.

5. Bake for 8 to 10 minutes or until set. (Cookies do not brown.) Cool completely.

6. Dip half of each cookie into chocolate; sprinkle remaining half with powdered sugar. Refrigerate until set.

Makes about 3 dozen cookies

Pecan Crunchies

1 package DUNCAN HINES®
    Golden Sugar Cookie Mix
1 egg
1 tablespoon water
1½ cups crushed potato chips,
    divided
½ cup chopped pecans

1. Preheat oven to 375°F. Grease cookie sheets lightly.

2. Combine cookie mix, contents of buttery flavor packet from Mix, egg, water, ½ cup potato chips and pecans in large bowl. Stir until thoroughly blended. Form dough into 36 (1-inch) balls. Roll in remaining 1 cup crushed potato chips. Place, 2 inches apart, on cookie sheets. Flatten dough with fork.

3. Bake at 375°F for 8 to 10 minutes or until golden brown. Cool 1 minute on cookie sheets. Remove to cooling racks. Cool completely. Store in airtight container.

Makes about 3 dozen cookies

Snickerdoodles

3 tablespoons sugar
1 teaspoon ground cinnamon
1 package (18.25 ounces)
    DUNCAN HINES® Moist
    Deluxe Yellow Cake Mix
2 eggs
¼ cup CRISCO® Oil

1. Preheat oven to 375°F. Grease cookie sheet.

2. Combine sugar and cinnamon in small bowl.

3. Combine cake mix, eggs and Crisco® Oil in large bowl. Stir until well blended. Shape dough into 1-inch balls. Roll in cinnamon-sugar mixture. Place balls, 2 inches apart, on cookie sheet. Flatten balls with bottom of glass.

4. Bake at 375°F for 8 to 9 minutes or until set. Cool one minute on cookie sheet before removing to wire rack.

Makes about 3 dozen cookies

Top to bottom: Snickerdoodles and Pecan Crunchies

OLD WORLD PFEFFERNÜSSE COOKIES

½ **cup butter, softened**
¾ **cup packed brown sugar**
½ **cup molasses**
 1 **egg**
 1 **tablespoon licorice-flavored**
   liqueur (optional)
3¼ **cups all-purpose flour**
 1 **teaspoon baking soda**
 1 **teaspoon ground cinnamon**
½ **teaspoon ground cloves**
¼ **teaspoon ground nutmeg**
   Dash pepper
   Powdered sugar

Preheat oven to 350°F. Grease cookie sheets. Beat butter and brown sugar in large bowl until creamy. Beat in molasses, egg and liqueur, if desired, until light and fluffy. Mix in flour, baking soda, cinnamon, cloves, nutmeg and pepper. Shape level tablespoonfuls of dough into balls. Place 2 inches apart onto prepared cookie sheets.

Bake 12 to 14 minutes until set. Cool 2 minutes on cookie sheets. Remove to wire racks; sprinkle with powdered sugar. Cool completely. Store in airtight containers.

Makes about 4 dozen cookies

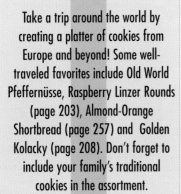

Take a trip around the world by creating a platter of cookies from Europe and beyond! Some well-traveled favorites include Old World Pfeffernüsse, Raspberry Linzer Rounds (page 203), Almond-Orange Shortbread (page 257) and Golden Kolacky (page 208). Don't forget to include your family's traditional cookies in the assortment.

Old World Pfeffernüsse Cookies

Festive Fudge Blossoms

¼ **cup butter, softened**
1 **box (18.25 ounces)
chocolate fudge cake mix**
1 **egg, slightly beaten**
2 **tablespoons water**
¾ **to 1 cup finely chopped
walnuts**
48 **chocolate star candies**

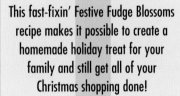

This fast-fixin' Festive Fudge Blossoms recipe makes it possible to create a homemade holiday treat for your family and still get all of your Christmas shopping done!

1. Preheat oven to 350°F. Cut butter into cake mix in large bowl until mixture resembles coarse crumbs. Stir in egg and water until well blended.

2. Shape dough into ½-inch balls; roll in walnuts, pressing nuts gently into dough. Place about 2 inches apart onto ungreased baking sheets.

3. Bake cookies 12 minutes or until puffed and nearly set. Place chocolate star in center of each cookie; bake 1 minute more. Cool 2 minutes on baking sheet. Remove cookies from baking sheets to wire rack to cool completely.

Makes 4 dozen cookies

Festive Fudge Blossoms

235

Tiny Mini Kisses Peanut Blossoms

½ cup shortening
¾ cup REESE'S® Creamy
    Peanut Butter
⅓ cup granulated sugar
⅓ cup packed light brown
    sugar
1 egg
3 tablespoons milk
1 teaspoon vanilla extract
1½ cups all-purpose flour
½ teaspoon baking soda
½ teaspoon salt
    Granulated sugar
    HERSHEY'S® MINI KISSES™
    Chocolate

1. Heat oven to 350°F.

2. In large bowl, beat shortening and peanut butter with electric mixer until well mixed. Add ⅓ cup granulated sugar and brown sugar; beat well. Add egg, milk and vanilla; beat until fluffy. Stir together flour, baking soda and salt; gradually add to peanut butter mixture, beating until blended. Shape into ½-inch balls. Roll in granulated sugar; place on ungreased cookie sheet.

3. Bake 5 to 6 minutes or until set. Immediately press MINI KISS™ Chocolate into center of each cookie. Remove from cookie sheet to wire rack.

Makes about 14 dozen cookies

Variation: For larger cookies, shape dough into 1-inch balls. Roll in granulated sugar. Place on ungreased cookie sheet. Bake 10 minutes or until set. Immediately place 3 MINI KISSES™ Chocolate in center of each cookie, pressing down slightly. Remove from cookie sheet to wire rack. Cool completely.

Tiny Mini Kisses Peanut Blossoms

Chocolate Sugar Cookies

3 squares BAKER'S®
    Unsweetened Chocolate
1 cup (2 sticks) margarine or
    butter
1 cup sugar
1 egg
1 teaspoon vanilla
2 cups all-purpose flour
1 teaspoon baking soda
¼ teaspoon salt
    Additional sugar

MICROWAVE chocolate and margarine in large microwavable bowl on HIGH 2 minutes or until margarine is melted. Stir until chocolate is completely melted.

STIR 1 cup sugar into melted chocolate mixture until well blended. Stir in egg and vanilla until completely blended. Mix in flour, baking soda and salt. Refrigerate 30 minutes.

HEAT oven to 375°F. Shape dough into 1-inch balls; roll in additional sugar. Place, 2 inches apart, on ungreased cookie sheets. (If flatter, crisper cookies are desired, flatten balls with bottom of drinking glass.)

BAKE 8 to 10 minutes or until set. Remove from cookie sheets to cool on wire racks. *Makes about 3½ dozen cookies*

Jam-Filled Chocolate Sugar Cookies: *Prepare Chocolate Sugar Cookie dough as directed. Roll in finely chopped nuts in place of sugar. Make indentation in each ball; fill center with your favorite jam. Bake as directed.*

Chocolate-Caramel Sugar Cookies: *Prepare Chocolate Sugar Cookie dough as directed. Roll in finely chopped nuts in place of sugar. Make indentation in each ball; bake as directed. Microwave 1 package (14 ounces) caramels with 2 tablespoons milk in microwavable bowl on HIGH 3 minutes or until melted, stirring after 2 minutes. Fill centers of cookies with caramel mixture. Drizzle with melted Baker's® Semi-Sweet Chocolate.*

CANDY CANE COOKIES

1¼ cups granulated sugar
1 Butter Flavor* CRISCO®
    Stick or 1 cup Butter
    Flavor CRISCO® all-
    vegetable shortening
2 eggs
¼ cup light corn syrup or
    regular pancake syrup
1 tablespoon vanilla
3 cups plus 4 tablespoons all-
    purpose flour, divided
¾ teaspoon baking powder
½ teaspoon baking soda
½ teaspoon salt
½ teaspoon red food color
¼ teaspoon peppermint
    extract

*Butter Flavor Crisco is artificially flavored.

1. Combine sugar and shortening in large bowl. Beat at medium speed of electric mixer until well blended. Add eggs, syrup and vanilla. Beat until well blended and fluffy.

2. Combine 3 cups flour, baking powder, baking soda and salt. Add gradually to creamed mixture at low speed. Mix until well blended.

3. Divide dough in half. Add red food color and peppermint extract to one half. Wrap each half in plastic wrap. Refrigerate several hours or overnight.

4. Heat oven to 375°F. Place sheets of foil on countertop for cooling cookies.

5. Roll 1 rounded teaspoonful plain dough with hands into a 6-inch rope on lightly floured surface. Repeat, using 1 teaspoonful red dough. Place ropes side by side. Twist together gently. Pinch ends to seal. Curve one end into the "hook" of a candy cane. Transfer to ungreased baking sheet with large pancake turner. Repeat with remaining dough. Place cookies 2 inches apart.

6. Bake one baking sheet at a time at 375°F for 7 to 9 minutes, or until just lightly browned. *Do not overbake.* Cool 2 minutes on baking sheet. Remove cookies to foil to cool completely.   *Makes about 4½ dozen cookies*

Mexican Chocolate Macaroons

MEXICAN CHOCOLATE MACAROONS

**1 package (8 ounces)
semisweet baking
chocolate, divided
1¾ cups plus ⅓ cup whole
almonds, divided
¾ cup sugar
1 teaspoon ground cinnamon
1 teaspoon vanilla
2 egg whites**

1. Preheat oven to 400°F. Grease baking sheets; set aside.

2. Place 5 squares of chocolate in food processor; process until coarsely chopped. Add 1¾ cups almonds and sugar; process using on/off pulsing action until mixture is finely ground. Add cinnamon, vanilla and egg whites; process just until mixture forms moist dough.

3. Form dough into 1-inch balls (dough will be sticky). Place about 2 inches apart onto prepared baking sheets. Press 1 almond on top of each cookie.

4. Bake 8 to 10 minutes or just until set. Cool 2 minutes on baking sheets. Remove cookies from baking sheets to wire rack to cool.

5. Heat remaining 3 squares chocolate in small saucepan over very low heat until melted. Spoon chocolate into small resealable plastic food storage bag. Cut small corner off bottom of bag with scissors. Drizzle chocolate over cookies. Allow cookies to stand until chocolate drizzle is set. Store in airtight containers. *Makes 3 dozen cookies*

CHOCO-CARAMEL DELIGHTS

½ cup (1 stick) butter or
    margarine, softened
⅔ cup sugar
1 egg, separated
2 tablespoons milk
1 teaspoon vanilla extract
1 cup all-purpose flour
⅓ cup HERSHEY'S Cocoa
¼ teaspoon salt
1 cup finely chopped pecans
    Caramel Filling (recipe
    follows)
½ cup HERSHEY'S Semi-Sweet
    Chocolate Chips
1 teaspoon shortening

In medium bowl, beat butter, sugar, egg yolk, milk and vanilla until blended. Stir together flour, cocoa and salt; blend into butter mixture. Refrigerate dough at least 1 hour or until firm enough to handle.

Heat oven to 350°F. Lightly grease cookie sheet. Beat egg white slightly. Shape dough into 1-inch balls. Dip each ball into egg white; roll in pecans to coat. Place on prepared cookie sheet. Press thumb gently in center of each ball. Bake 10 to 12 minutes or until set. While cookies are baking, prepare Caramel Filling. Remove cookies from oven; press center of each cookie again with thumb to make indentation. Immediately spoon about ½ teaspoon Caramel Filling in center of each cookie. Carefully remove from cookie sheets; cool on wire racks.

In small microwave-safe bowl, place chocolate chips and shortening. Microwave at HIGH (100%) 1 minute or until softened; stir. Allow to stand several minutes to finish melting; stir until smooth. Place wax paper under wire rack with cookies. Drizzle chocolate mixture over top of cookies.

Makes about 2 dozen cookies

CARAMEL FILLING:

In small saucepan, combine 14 unwrapped light caramels and 3 tablespoons whipping cream. Cook over low heat, stirring frequently, until caramels are melted and mixture is smooth.

Choco-Caramel Delights

243

CRISPY THUMBPRINT COOKIES

1 package (18.25 ounces) yellow cake mix
½ cup vegetable oil
1 egg
¼ cup water
3 cups crisp rice cereal, crushed
½ cup chopped walnuts
Raspberry or strawberry preserves or Andes mint candies, cut in half

1. Preheat oven to 375°F.

2. Combine cake mix, oil, egg and water. Beat at medium speed of electric mixer until well blended. Add cereal and walnuts; mix until well blended.

3. Drop by heaping teaspoonfuls about 2 inches apart onto ungreased baking sheets. Use thumb to make indentation in each cookie. Spoon about ½ teaspoon preserves into center of each cookie. (Or, place ½ of mint candy in center of each cookie.)

4. Bake 9 to 11 minutes or until golden brown. Cool cookies 1 minute on baking sheet; remove from baking sheet to wire rack to cool completely. *Makes 3 dozen cookies*

CHOCOLATE RASPBERRY THUMBPRINTS

1½ cups butter, softened
1 cup sugar
1 egg
1 teaspoon vanilla extract
3 cups all-purpose flour
¼ cup unsweetened cocoa
½ teaspoon salt
1 cup (6 ounces) semisweet mini chocolate chips
⅔ cup raspberry preserves
Powdered sugar (optional)

Preheat oven to 350°F. Grease cookie sheets. Beat butter and sugar in large bowl. Beat in egg and vanilla until light and fluffy. Mix in flour, cocoa and salt until well blended. Stir in chocolate chips. Roll level tablespoonfuls of dough into balls. Place 2 inches apart onto prepared cookie sheets. Make deep indentation in center of each ball with thumb.

Bake 12 to 15 minutes until just set. Cool 2 minutes on cookie sheets. Remove to wire racks; cool completely. Fill centers with raspberry preserves and sprinkle with powdered sugar, if desired. Store between layers of waxed paper in airtight containers. *Makes about 4½ dozen cookies*

Crispy Thumbprint Cookies

HOLIDAY FRUIT DROPS

¾ cup packed brown sugar
½ cup butter, softened
1 egg
1¼ cups all-purpose flour
1 teaspoon vanilla
½ teaspoon baking soda
½ teaspoon ground cinnamon
　Pinch salt
1 cup (8 ounces) diced
　candied pineapple
1 cup (8 ounces) whole red
　and green candied
　cherries
8 ounces chopped pitted dates
1 cup (6 ounces) semisweet
　chocolate chips
½ cup whole hazelnuts
½ cup pecan halves
½ cup coarsely chopped
　walnuts

Preheat oven to 325°F. Lightly grease cookie sheets. Beat sugar and butter in large bowl. Beat in egg until light and fluffy. Mix in flour, vanilla, baking soda, cinnamon and salt. Stir in pineapple, cherries, dates, chocolate chips, hazelnuts, pecans and walnuts. Drop dough by rounded teaspoonfuls 2 inches apart onto prepared cookie sheets.

Bake 15 to 20 minutes or until firm and lightly browned around edges. Remove to wire racks to cool completely.

Makes about 8 dozen cookies

Note: The cherries, hazelnuts and pecan halves are not chopped, but left whole.

CHOCOLATE CHERRY OATMEAL FANCIES

½ cup sliced almonds

1¼ cups firmly packed light brown sugar

¾ Butter Flavor* CRISCO® Stick or ¾ cup Butter Flavor* CRISCO® all-vegetable shortening

1 egg

⅓ cup milk

1 teaspoon vanilla

½ teaspoon almond extract

3 cups quick oats, uncooked

1 cup all-purpose flour

½ teaspoon baking soda

½ teaspoon salt

6 ounces white baking chocolate, coarsely chopped

6 ounces semisweet chocolate, coarsely chopped

½ cup coarsely chopped red candied cherries or well-drained, chopped maraschino cherries

*Butter Flavor Crisco is artificially flavored.

1. Heat oven to 350°F. Spread almonds on baking sheet. Bake at 350°F for 5 to 7 minutes or until almonds are golden brown. Cool completely; reserve.

2. Increase oven temperature to 375°F. Grease baking sheets with shortening. Place sheets of foil on countertop for cooling cookies.

3. Place brown sugar, shortening, egg, milk, vanilla and almond extract in large bowl. Beat at medium speed of electric mixer until well blended.

4. Combine oats, flour, baking soda and salt. Add to shortening mixture; beat at low speed just until blended. Stir in white chocolate, semisweet chocolate, cherries and reserved almonds.

5. Drop by rounded measuring tablespoonfuls 2 inches apart onto prepared baking sheets.

6. Bake one baking sheet at a time at 375°F for 10 to 12 minutes or until cookies are lightly browned. *Do not overbake.* Cool 2 minutes on baking sheet. Remove cookies to foil to cool completely.   *Makes about 4 dozen cookies*

Pumpkin White Chocolate Drops

2 cups butter, softened
2 cups granulated sugar
1 can (16 ounces) solid pack
    pumpkin
2 eggs
4 cups all-purpose flour
2 tablespoons pumpkin pie
    spice
1 teaspoon baking powder
½ teaspoon baking soda
1 bag (12 ounces) vanilla
    baking chips
1 container (16 ounces)
    ready-to-spread cream
    cheese frosting
¼ cup packed brown sugar

1. Preheat oven to 375°F. Beat butter and granulated sugar in large bowl until light and fluffy. Add pumpkin and eggs; beat until smooth. Add flour, pumpkin pie spice, baking powder and baking soda; beat just until well blended. Stir in baking chips.

2. Drop rounded tablespoonfuls of dough 2 inches apart onto greased cookie sheets; bake 14 to 18 minutes or until set and bottoms are brown. Cool 1 minute on baking sheets. Remove from baking sheets to wire rack to cool.

3. Combine frosting and brown sugar in small bowl. Spread on warm cookies.   *Makes about 6 dozen cookies*

Chocolate Clouds

3 egg whites, at room
    temperature
⅛ teaspoon cream of tartar
¾ cup sugar
1 teaspoon vanilla extract
2 tablespoons HERSHEY'S
    Cocoa
2 cups (12-ounce package)
    HERSHEY'S Semi-Sweet
    Chocolate Chips

Heat oven to 300°F. Cover cookie sheet with parchment paper or foil. In large bowl, beat egg whites and cream of tartar at high speed of electric mixer until soft peaks form. Gradually add sugar and vanilla, beating well after each addition until stiff peaks hold, sugar is dissolved and mixture is glossy. Sift cocoa onto egg white mixture; gently fold just until combined. Fold in chocolate chips. Drop by heaping tablespoons onto prepared cookie sheet. Bake 35 to 45 minutes or just until dry. Cool slightly; peel paper from cookies. Store, covered, at room temperature.

Makes 30 cookies

Pumpkin White Chocolate Drops

FRUITCAKE COOKIES

¾ **cup sugar**
½ **cup butter, softened**
1 **egg**
½ **cup milk**
2 **tablespoons orange juice**
1 **tablespoon vinegar**
2 **cups all-purpose flour**
1 **teaspoon baking powder**
½ **teaspoon baking soda**
¼ **teaspoon salt**
½ **cup chopped walnuts**
½ **cup chopped candied mixed fruit**
½ **cup raisins**
¼ **cup chopped dried pineapple**
   Powdered sugar

Preheat oven to 350°F. Grease cookie sheets. Beat sugar and butter in large bowl until fluffy. Beat in egg, milk, orange juice and vinegar until blended. Mix in flour, baking powder, baking soda and salt. Stir in walnuts, mixed fruit, raisins and pineapple. Drop rounded tablespoonfuls of dough 2 inches apart onto prepared cookie sheets.

Bake 12 to 14 minutes until lightly browned around edges. Cool 2 minutes on cookie sheets. Remove to wire racks; cool completely. Dust with powdered sugar. Store in airtight container. *Makes about 2½ dozen cookies*

Fruitcake Cookies

PEANUT BUTTER CHIP TASSIES

1 package (3 ounces) cream cheese, softened
½ cup (1 stick) butter, softened
1 cup all-purpose flour
1 egg, slightly beaten
½ cup sugar
2 tablespoons butter, melted
¼ teaspoon lemon juice
¼ teaspoon vanilla extract
1 cup REESE'S® Peanut Butter Chips, chopped*
6 red candied cherries, quartered (optional)

Do not chop peanut butter chips in food processor or blender.

1. In medium bowl, beat cream cheese and ½ cup butter; stir in flour. Cover; refrigerate about one hour or until dough is firm. Shape into 24 one-inch balls; place each ball into ungreased, small muffin cups (1¾ inches in diameter). Press dough evenly against bottom and sides of each cup.

2. Heat oven to 350°F.

3. In medium bowl, combine egg, sugar, melted butter, lemon juice and vanilla; stir until smooth. Add chopped peanut butter chips. Fill muffin cups ¾ full with mixture.

4. Bake 20 to 25 minutes or until filling is set and lightly browned. Cool completely; remove from pan to wire rack. Garnish with candied cherries, if desired.

Makes about 2 dozen

Peanut Butter Chip Tassies

CHOCOLATE PECAN TASSIES

CRUST
- ½ cup (1 stick) margarine or butter
- 1 package (3 ounces) PHILADELPHIA BRAND® Cream Cheese, softened
- 1 cup all-purpose flour

FILLING
- 1 square BAKER'S® Unsweetened Chocolate
- 1 tablespoon margarine or butter
- ¾ cup packed brown sugar
- 1 egg
- 1 teaspoon vanilla extract
- 1 cup chopped pecans
- Powdered sugar (optional)

BEAT ½ cup margarine and cream cheese until well blended. Beat in flour until just blended. Wrap dough in plastic wrap; refrigerate 1 hour.

HEAT oven to 350°F. Microwave chocolate and 1 tablespoon margarine in large microwavable bowl on HIGH 1 minute or until margarine is melted. Stir until chocolate is completely melted.

BEAT in brown sugar, egg and vanilla until thickened. Stir in pecans.

SHAPE chilled dough into 36 (1-inch) balls. Flatten each ball and press onto bottoms and up sides of ungreased miniature muffin cups. Spoon about 1 teaspoon filling into each cup.

BAKE 20 minutes. Cool in pans on wire racks 15 minutes. Remove from pans. Sprinkle with powdered sugar.

Makes 36 tassies

KENTUCKY BOURBON PECAN TARTS

**Cream Cheese Pastry
(recipe follows)**
2 eggs
½ cup granulated sugar
**½ cup KARO® Light or Dark
Corn Syrup**
2 tablespoons bourbon
**1 tablespoon MAZOLA®
Margarine, melted**
½ teaspoon vanilla
1 cup chopped pecans
**Confectioners' sugar
(optional)**

1. Preheat oven to 350°F. Prepare Cream Cheese Pastry. Divide dough in half; set aside 1 half.

2. On floured surface roll out pastry to ⅛-inch thickness. If necessary, add small amount of flour to keep pastry from sticking. Cut into 12 (2¼-inch) rounds. Press evenly into bottoms and up sides of 1¾-inch muffin pan cups. Repeat with remaining pastry. Refrigerate.

3. In medium bowl, beat eggs slightly. Stir in granulated sugar, corn syrup, bourbon, margarine and vanilla until well blended. Spoon 1 heaping teaspoon pecans into each pastry-lined cup; top with 1 tablespoon corn syrup mixture.

4. Bake 20 to 25 minutes or until lightly browned and toothpick inserted into center comes out clean. Cool in pans 5 minutes. Remove; cool completely on wire rack. If desired, sprinkle cookies with confectioners' sugar.

Makes about 2 dozen cookies

CREAM CHEESE PASTRY

1 cup all-purpose flour
¾ teaspoon baking powder
Pinch salt
½ cup MAZOLA® Margarine, softened
1 package (3 ounces) cream cheese, softened
2 teaspoons sugar

1. In small bowl, combine flour, baking powder and salt.

2. In large bowl, mix margarine, cream cheese and sugar until well combined. Stir in flour mixture until well blended. Press firmly into ball with hands.

Almond-Orange Shortbread

ALMOND-ORANGE SHORTBREAD

1 cup (4 ounces) sliced almonds, divided
2 cups all-purpose flour
1 cup cold butter, cut into pieces
½ cup sugar
½ cup cornstarch
2 tablespoons grated orange peel
1 teaspoon almond extract

1. Preheat oven to 350°F. To toast almonds, spread ¾ cup almonds in single layer in large baking pan. Bake 6 minutes or until golden brown, stirring frequently. Remove almonds from oven. Cool completely in pan. Reduce oven temperature to 325°F.

2. Place almonds in food processor. Process using on/off pulsing action until almonds are coarsely chopped. Add flour, butter, sugar, cornstarch, orange peel and almond extract. Process using on/off pulsing action until mixture resembles coarse crumbs.

3. Press dough firmly and evenly into 10½×8½-inch rectangle on large ungreased baking sheet. Score dough into 1¼-inch squares. Press one slice of remaining ¼ cup almonds in center of each square.

4. Bake 30 to 40 minutes or until shortbread is firm when pressed and lightly browned. Immediately cut into squares along score lines. Remove cookies with spatula to wire racks; cool completely. Store loosely covered at room temperature up to 1 week.   *Makes 5 dozen cookies*

Cashew-Lemon Shortbread Cookies

½ cup roasted cashews
1 cup butter, softened
½ cup sugar
2 teaspoons lemon extract
1 teaspoon vanilla
2 cups all-purpose flour

1. Preheat oven to 325°F. Place cashews in food processor; process until finely ground. Add butter, sugar, lemon extract and vanilla; process until well blended. Add flour; process using on/off pulsing action until dough is well blended and begins to form ball.

2. Shape dough into 1½-inch balls; roll in additional sugar. Place about 2 inches apart onto ungreased baking sheets; flatten with bottom of glass.

3. Bake cookies 17 to 19 minutes or just until set and edges are lightly browned. Remove cookies from baking sheets to wire rack to cool.   *Makes 2 to 2½ dozen cookies*

Chocolate Almond Shortbread

¾ cup (1½ sticks) butter or
    margarine, softened
1¼ cups powdered sugar
6 squares BAKER'S® Semi-
    Sweet Chocolate, melted,
    cooled
1 teaspoon vanilla
1 cup all-purpose flour
1 cup toasted ground
    blanched almonds
¼ teaspoon salt
½ cup toasted chopped
    almonds

HEAT oven to 250°F.

BEAT butter and sugar until light and fluffy. Stir in chocolate and vanilla. Mix in flour, ground almonds and salt.

PRESS dough into 12×9-inch rectangle on ungreased cookie sheet. Sprinkle with chopped almonds; press lightly into dough.

BAKE for 45 to 50 minutes or until set. Cool on cookie sheet; cut into bars.   *Makes about 36 bars*

Cashew-Lemon Shortbread Cookies

FESTIVE FRUITED WHITE CHIP BLONDIES

½ cup (1 stick) butter or margarine

1⅔ cups (10-ounce package) HERSHEY'S Premier White Chips, divided

2 eggs

¼ cup granulated sugar

1¼ cups all-purpose flour

⅓ cup orange juice

¾ cup cranberries, chopped

¼ cup chopped dried apricots

½ cup coarsely chopped nuts

¼ cup packed light brown sugar

1. Heat oven to 325°F. Grease and flour 9-inch square baking pan.

2. In medium saucepan, melt butter; stir in 1 cup white chips. In large bowl, beat eggs until foamy. Add granulated sugar; beat until thick and pale yellow in color. Add flour, orange juice and white chip mixture; beat just until combined. Spread one-half of batter, about 1¼ cups, into prepared pan.

3. Bake 15 minutes until edges are lightly browned; remove from oven.

4. Stir cranberries, apricots and remaining ⅔ cup white chips into remaining one-half of batter; spread over top of hot baked mixture. Stir together nuts and brown sugar; sprinkle over top.

5. Bake 25 to 30 minutes or until edges are lightly browned. Cool completely in pan on wire rack. Cut into bars.

Makes about 16 bars

Festive Fruited White Chip Blondies

261

Double Chocolate Fantasy Bars

2 cups chocolate cookie crumbs

⅓ cup (5⅓ tablespoons) butter or margarine, melted

1 14-ounce can sweetened condensed milk

1¾ cups "M&M's"® Semi-Sweet Chocolate Mini Baking Bits

1 cup shredded coconut

1 cup chopped walnuts or pecans

Preheat oven to 350°F. In large bowl combine cookie crumbs and butter; press mixture onto bottom of 13×9×2-inch baking pan. Pour condensed milk evenly over crumbs. Combine "M&M's"® Semi-Sweet Chocolate Mini Baking Bits, coconut and nuts. Sprinkle mixture evenly over condensed milk; press down lightly. Bake 25 to 30 minutes or until set. Cool completely. Cut into bars. Store in tightly covered container. *Makes 32 bars*

Rainbow Blondies

1 cup (2 sticks) butter or margarine, softened

1½ cups firmly packed light brown sugar

1 large egg

1 teaspoon vanilla extract

2 cups all-purpose flour

½ teaspoon baking soda

1¾ cups "M&M's"® Semi-Sweet or Milk Chocolate Mini Baking Bits

1 cup chopped walnuts or pecans

Preheat oven to 350°F. Lightly grease 13×9×2-inch baking pan; set aside. In large bowl cream butter and sugar until light and fluffy; beat in egg and vanilla. In medium bowl combine flour and baking soda; add to creamed mixture just until combined. Dough will be stiff. Stir in "M&M's"® Chocolate Mini Baking Bits and nuts. Spread dough into prepared baking pan. Bake 30 to 35 minutes or until toothpick inserted in center comes out with moist crumbs. Do not overbake. Cool completely. Cut into bars. Store in tightly covered container. *Makes 24 bars*

Left to right: Double Chocolate Fantasy Bars and Rainbow Blondies

ALMOND TOFFEE TRIANGLES

Bar Cookie Crust (recipe follows)
⅓ cup KARO® Light or Dark Corn Syrup
⅓ cup packed brown sugar
3 tablespoons MAZOLA® Margarine or butter
¼ cup heavy or whipping cream
1½ cups sliced almonds
1 teaspoon vanilla

1. Preheat oven to 350°F. Prepare Bar Cookie Crust.

2. Meanwhile, in medium saucepan combine corn syrup, brown sugar, margarine and cream. Bring to boil over medium heat; remove from heat. Stir in almonds and vanilla. Pour over hot crust; spread evenly.

3. Bake 12 minutes or until set and golden. Cool completely on wire rack. Cut into 2-inch squares; cut diagonally in half for triangles.   *Makes about 48 triangles*

BAR COOKIE CRUST

MAZOLA NO STICK® Cooking Spray
2 cups flour
½ cup (1 stick) cold MAZOLA® Margarine or butter, cut into pieces
⅓ cup sugar
¼ teaspoon salt

1. Preheat oven to 350°F. Spray 13×9-inch baking pan with cooking spray.

2. In large bowl with mixer at medium speed, beat flour, margarine, sugar and salt until mixture resembles coarse crumbs. Press firmly into bottom and ¼ inch up sides of prepared pan.

3. Bake 15 minutes or until golden brown. Top with desired filling. Complete as recipe directs.

Clockwise from top: Pecan Pie Bars (page 276), Almond Toffee Triangles and Chocolate Chip Walnut Bars (page 266)

Chocolate Chip Walnut Bars

**Bar Cookie Crust
(page 264)**
2 eggs
**½ cup KARO® Light or Dark
Corn Syrup**
½ cup sugar
**2 tablespoons MAZOLA®
Margarine or butter,
melted**
**1 cup (6 oz) semisweet
chocolate chips**
¾ cup chopped walnuts

1. Preheat oven to 350°F. Prepare Bar Cookie Crust.

2. Meanwhile, in medium bowl beat eggs, corn syrup, sugar and margarine until well blended. Stir in chocolate chips and walnuts. Pour over hot crust; spread evenly.

3. Bake 15 to 18 minutes or until set. Cool completely on wire rack. Cut into 2×1½-inch bars.

Makes about 32 bars

Sensational Peppermint Pattie Brownies

**24 small (1½-inch) YORK®
Peppermint Patties**
**1½ cups (3 sticks) butter or
margarine, melted**
3 cups sugar
1 tablespoon vanilla extract
5 eggs
2 cups all-purpose flour
1 cup HERSHEY'S Cocoa
1 teaspoon baking powder
1 teaspoon salt

Heat oven to 350°F. Remove wrappers from peppermint patties. Grease 13×9×2-inch baking pan. In large bowl, stir together butter, sugar and vanilla. Add eggs; beat until well blended. Stir together flour, cocoa, baking powder and salt; gradually add to butter mixture, blending well. Reserve 2 cups batter. Spread remaining batter into prepared pan. Arrange peppermint patties about ½ inch apart in single layer over batter. Spread reserved batter over patties. Bake 50 to 55 minutes or until brownies pull away from sides of pan. Cool completely in pan on wire rack. *About 36 brownies*

Santa's Favorite Brownies

1 cup (6 ounces) milk
  chocolate chips
½ cup butter
¾ cup sugar
2 eggs
1 teaspoon vanilla extract
1¼ cups all-purpose flour
3 tablespoons unsweetened
  cocoa
1 teaspoon baking powder
½ teaspoon salt
½ cup chopped walnuts
  Buttercream Frosting
  (recipe follows), optional
  Small jelly beans, icing gels
  and colored sugar for
  decoration (optional)

Preheat oven to 350°F. Grease 9-inch square baking pan. Melt chocolate and butter with sugar in medium saucepan over low heat, stirring constantly. Pour into large bowl; add eggs and vanilla. Beat with electric mixer until well blended. Stir in flour, cocoa, baking powder and salt; blend well. Fold in walnuts. Spread into prepared pan.

Bake 25 to 30 minutes or until wooden toothpick inserted in center comes out clean. Place pan on wire rack; cool completely. Frost with Buttercream Frosting, if desired. Cut into squares. Decorate with jelly beans, icing gels and colored sugar, if desired. Store in airtight container.

Makes 16 brownies

Buttercream Frosting

3 cups powdered sugar, sifted
½ cup butter, softened
3 to 4 tablespoons milk, divided
½ teaspoon vanilla extract

Combine powdered sugar, butter, 2 tablespoons milk and vanilla in large bowl. Beat with electric mixer on low speed until blended. Beat on high speed until light and fluffy, adding more milk, 1 teaspoon at a time, as needed for good spreading consistency.   *Makes about 1½ cups frosting*

267

Chocolate Nut Bars

Chocolate Nut Bars

½ cup uncooked quick oats
½ cup hazelnuts
½ cup toasted walnuts
¾ cup powdered sugar
8 ounces (1¼ cups) semisweet chocolate chips
1 tablespoon vegetable shortening
2 tablespoons butter
½ teaspoon salt
⅓ cup corn syrup
½ teaspoon vanilla

1. Preheat oven to 350°F. Line an 8-inch square baking pan with foil, pressing foil into corners to cover completely and leaving 1-inch overhang on sides.

2. Spread oats on baking sheet. Bake 8 to 10 minutes or until light golden brown. Transfer oats to large bowl when cool. Reduce oven temperature to 325°F. Chop hazelnuts into uniform pieces. Spread on baking sheet. Bake 9 to 11 minutes or just until cut sides begin to brown lightly. Transfer to bowl with toasted oats when cool. Chop walnuts into uniform pieces; add to oat mixture. Stir in powdered sugar; set aside.

3. Heat chocolate chips with shortening in heavy small saucepan over very low heat, stirring constantly, until melted and smooth. Remove from heat. Spread evenly onto bottom of prepared pan with rubber spatula. Let stand in cool place about 15 to 20 minutes or until it begins to set, but is not firm.

4. Combine butter and salt in microwavable bowl. Microwave at HIGH 45 to 55 seconds or until butter is melted and foamy. Stir in corn syrup. After cooling slightly, stir vanilla into oat mixture just until moistened. Gently spoon over chocolate, spreading evenly into corners with rubber spatula. Score lightly into 4 strips, then score each strip into 6 pieces. Cover tightly with plastic wrap and refrigerate until firm, at least 4 hours.

5. Remove from pan by lifting foil by edges. Place on cutting board; cut along score lines into 24 pieces. Remove from foil. Store in airtight container in refrigerator.   *Makes 24 bars*

APPLE CRUMB SQUARES

2 cups QUAKER® Oats (quick or old fashioned, uncooked)
1½ cups all-purpose flour
1 cup packed brown sugar
¾ cup butter or margarine, melted
1 teaspoon ground cinnamon
½ teaspoon baking soda
½ teaspoon salt (optional)
¼ teaspoon ground nutmeg
1 cup applesauce
½ cup chopped nuts

Preheat oven to 350°F. In large bowl, combine all ingredients except applesauce and nuts; mix until crumbly. Reserve 1 cup oats mixture. Press remaining mixture on bottom of greased 13×9-inch pan. Bake 13 to 15 minutes; cool. Spread applesauce over partially baked crust; sprinkle with nuts. Sprinkle reserved 1 cup oats mixture over top. Bake 13 to 15 minutes or until golden brown. Cool in pan on wire rack; cut into 2-inch squares. *Makes about 24 squares*

PEANUTTY CHOCOLATE CHIP BARS

1 cup SKIPPY® SUPER CHUNK® or Creamy Peanut Butter
1 cup packed brown sugar
⅔ cup KARO® Light or Dark Corn Syrup
½ cup MAZOLA® Margarine, softened
2 eggs
1 teaspoon vanilla
2½ cups flour
1½ teaspoons baking powder
½ teaspoon salt
2 cups (12 ounces) semisweet chocolate chips, divided

1. Preheat oven to 350°F.

2. In large bowl with mixer at medium speed, beat peanut butter, brown sugar, corn syrup, margarine, eggs and vanilla until smooth. Reduce speed; beat in flour, baking powder and salt until well blended. Stir in 1½ cups chocolate chips. Spread evenly in ungreased 15×10×1-inch baking pan.

3. Bake 25 minutes or until lightly browned. Cool completely on wire rack.

4. In small heavy saucepan over low heat, stir remaining ½ cup chocolate chips until melted and smooth. Drizzle over surface; cool before cutting. *Makes 48 bars*

Apple Crumb Squares

271

GERMAN SWEET CHOCOLATE CREAM CHEESE BROWNIES

BROWNIE LAYER:
   1 package (4 ounces)
      BAKER'S® GERMAN'S
      Sweet Chocolate
   ¼ cup (½ stick) margarine or
      butter
   ¾ cup sugar
   2 eggs
   1 teaspoon vanilla
   ½ cup all-purpose flour
   ½ cup chopped nuts

CREAM CHEESE LAYER:
   4 ounces PHILADELPHIA
      BRAND® Cream Cheese,
      softened
   ¼ cup sugar
   1 egg
   1 tablespoon all-purpose flour

HEAT oven to 350°F.

MICROWAVE chocolate and margarine in large microwavable bowl on HIGH 2 minutes or until margarine is melted. Stir until chocolate is completely melted.

STIR ¾ cup sugar into melted chocolate mixture. Mix in 2 eggs and vanilla until well blended. Stir in ½ cup flour and nuts. Spread in greased 8-inch square pan.

MIX cream cheese, ¼ cup sugar, 1 egg and 1 tablespoon flour in same bowl until smooth. Place spoonfuls over brownie batter. Swirl with knife to marbleize.

BAKE for 35 minutes or until toothpick inserted into center comes out with fudgy crumbs. Do not overbake. Cool in pan; cut into squares. *Makes about 16 brownies*

Easy Linzer Bars

2 cups flour
½ cup sugar
¾ teaspoon baking soda
½ teaspoon cinnamon
½ teaspoon grated lemon peel
½ cup (1 stick) MAZOLA®
    Margarine or butter
¼ cup KARO® Light Corn
    Syrup
½ cup seedless raspberry
    preserves
⅓ cup finely chopped walnuts
⅔ cup confectioners sugar
1 tablespoon milk

1. Preheat oven to 350°F. In large bowl combine flour, sugar, baking soda, cinnamon and lemon peel.

2. In small saucepan heat margarine and corn syrup over low heat until margarine melts. Stir into flour mixture until blended. Divide dough into 5 equal pieces.

3. On large ungreased cookie sheet, pat each piece of dough into 14×1-inch rope.

4. Combine raspberry preserves and walnuts. Make an indentation down center of each rope; fill with preserve mixture, mounding slightly.

5. Bake 12 to 14 minutes or until lightly browned. Remove from oven; immediately cut diagonally into 1-inch-wide slices.

6. In small bowl stir confectioners sugar and milk until smooth. Drizzle over warm cookies. Cool on wire racks. Store in airtight container. *Makes about 5 dozen cookies*

CHIPPY CHEWY BARS

½ cup (1 stick) butter or margarine
1½ cups graham cracker crumbs
1⅔ cups (10-ounce package) REESE'S® Peanut Butter Chips, divided
1½ cups MOUNDS™ Sweetened Coconut Flakes
1 can (14 ounces) sweetened condensed milk (not evaporated milk)
1 cup HERSHEY'S Semi-Sweet Chocolate Chips or HERSHEY'S MINI CHIPS™ Semi-Sweet Chocolate
1½ teaspoons shortening (do not use butter, margarine or oil)

1. Heat oven to 350°F.

2. Place butter in 13×9×2-inch baking pan. Heat in oven until melted. Remove pan from oven. Sprinkle graham cracker crumbs evenly over butter; press down with fork. Layer 1 cup peanut butter chips over crumbs; sprinkle coconut over peanut butter chips. Layer remaining ⅔ cup peanut butter chips over coconut; drizzle sweetened condensed milk evenly over top.

3. Bake 20 minutes or until lightly browned.

4. In small microwave-safe bowl, place chocolate chips and shortening. Microwave at HIGH (100%) 1 minute; stir. If necessary, microwave at HIGH an additional 15 seconds at a time, stirring after each heating, just until chips are melted when stirred. Drizzle evenly over top of baked mixture. Cool completely in pan on wire rack. Cut into bars.

Makes about 48 bars

Note: For lighter drizzle, use ½ cup chocolate chips and ¾ teaspoon shortening. Microwave at HIGH 30 seconds to 1 minute; stir. If necessary, microwave at HIGH an additional 15 seconds at a time, stirring after each heating, just until chips are melted when stirred.

Chippy Chewy Bars

CINNAMONY APPLE STREUSEL BARS

1¼ cups graham cracker crumbs
1¼ cups all-purpose flour
¾ cup packed brown sugar, divided
¼ cup granulated sugar
1 teaspoon ground cinnamon
¾ cup butter or margarine, melted
2 cups chopped apples (2 medium apples, cored and peeled)
Glaze (recipe follows)

Preheat oven to 350°F. Grease 13×9-inch baking pan. Combine graham cracker crumbs, flour, ½ cup brown sugar, granulated sugar and cinnamon in large bowl. Stir in melted butter until well blended; reserve 1 cup. Press remaining crumb mixture into bottom of prepared pan.

Bake 8 minutes. Remove from oven; set aside. Toss apples with remaining ¼ cup brown sugar in medium bowl until brown sugar is dissolved; arrange apples over baked crust. Sprinkle reserved 1 cup crumb mixture over filling. Bake 30 to 35 minutes more or until apples are tender. Remove pan to wire rack; cool completely. Drizzle with Glaze. Cut into bars.

Makes 3 dozen bars

GLAZE:

Combine ½ cup powdered sugar and 1 tablespoon milk in small bowl until well blended.

PECAN PIE BARS

Bar Cookie Crust (page 264)
2 eggs
¾ cup KARO® Light or Dark Corn Syrup
¾ cup sugar
2 tablespoons MAZOLA® Margarine or butter, melted
1 teaspoon vanilla
1¼ cups coarsely chopped pecans

1. Preheat oven to 350°F. Prepare Bar Cookie Crust.

2. Meanwhile, in large bowl beat eggs, corn syrup, sugar, margarine and vanilla until well blended. Stir in pecans. Pour over hot crust; spread evenly.

3. Bake 20 minutes or until filling is firm around edges and slightly firm in center. Cool completely on wire rack. Cut into 2×1½-inch bars.

Makes about 32 bars

Cinnamony Apple Streusel Bars

Chocolate Cream Cheese Brownies

1 cup (2 sticks) butter or
    margarine, softened
1 package (3 ounces) cream
    cheese, softened
2 cups sugar
3 eggs
1 teaspoon vanilla extract
1 cup all-purpose flour
¾ cup HERSHEY'S Cocoa
¼ teaspoon baking powder
½ teaspoon salt
¾ cup chopped nuts
    Brownie Frosting (recipe
    follows)

Heat oven to 325°F. Grease bottom of 13×9×2-inch baking pan. In large mixer bowl, beat butter, cream cheese and sugar until light and fluffy. Add eggs and vanilla; beat well. Stir together flour, cocoa, baking powder and salt; gradually add to butter mixture, blending well. Stir in nuts. Spread batter into prepared pan. Bake 35 to 40 minutes or just until brownies begin to pull away from sides of pan. Cool completely in pan on wire rack. Prepare Brownie Frosting; spread over brownies. Cut into bars.

Makes about 36 brownies

Brownie Frosting

3 tablespoons butter or margarine, softened
3 tablespoons HERSHEY'S Cocoa
1⅓ cups powdered sugar
¾ teaspoon vanilla extract
1 tablespoon milk
1 tablespoon light corn syrup (optional)

In small bowl, beat butter and cocoa until blended; gradually add powdered sugar and vanilla, beating well. Add milk and corn syrup, if desired; beat until smooth and of spreading consistency. Add additional milk, ½ teaspoon at a time, if needed.

Top to bottom: Sensational Peppermint Pattie Brownies (page 266), Brownies with Peanut Butter Chips (page 280) and Chocolate Cream Cheese Brownies

Brownies with Peanut Butter Chips

1¼ cups (2½ sticks) butter or margarine, melted
1¾ cups sugar
4 eggs
2 teaspoons vanilla extract
1⅔ cups all-purpose flour
⅔ cup HERSHEY'S Cocoa
½ teaspoon baking powder
½ teaspoon salt
1⅔ cups (10-ounce package) REESE'S® Peanut Butter Chips, divided
Peanut Butter Chip Glaze (recipe follows)

Heat oven to 350°F. Grease 13×9×2-inch baking pan. In large bowl, stir together butter and sugar. Add eggs and vanilla; beat with spoon or whisk until well blended. Stir together flour, cocoa, baking powder and salt; gradually add to butter mixture, stirring until well blended. Reserve ½ cup peanut butter chips for glaze; stir remaining chips into batter. Spread batter into prepared pan. Bake 30 to 35 minutes or until wooden pick inserted in center comes out clean. Cool completely in pan on wire rack. Prepare Peanut Butter Chip Glaze; drizzle over brownies. Let stand until glaze is set. Cut into squares. *Makes about 32 brownies*

Peanut Butter Chip Glaze

½ cup REESE'S® Peanut Butter Chips (reserved from brownies)
2 tablespoons butter or margarine
2 tablespoons milk
¼ cup powdered sugar

In small microwave-safe bowl, place peanut butter chips, butter and milk. Microwave at HIGH (100%) 45 seconds; stir. If necessary, microwave at HIGH an additional 15 seconds at a time, stirring after each heating, just until chips are melted when stirred. Gradually add powdered sugar, beating with whisk until smooth.

PEANUT BUTTER CRISPY TREATS

4 cups toasted rice cereal
1¾ cups "M&M's"® Milk
    Chocolate Mini Baking
    Bits
4 cups mini marshmallows
½ cup creamy peanut butter
¼ cup butter or margarine
⅛ teaspoon salt

Combine cereal and "M&M's"® Milk Chocolate Mini Baking Bits in lightly greased baking pan; set aside. Melt marshmallows, peanut butter, butter and salt in heavy saucepan over low heat, stirring occasionally until mixture is smooth. Pour melted mixture over cereal mixture, tossing lightly until thoroughly coated. Gently shape into 1½-inch balls with buttered fingers. Place on waxed paper; cool at room temperature until set. Store in tightly covered container.

Makes about 3 dozen

Variation: After cereal mixture is thoroughly coated, press lightly into greased 13×9×2-inch pan. Cool completely; cut into bars.   *Makes 24 bars*

CHOCOLATE PECAN PIE BARS

Bar Cookie Crust
    (page 264)
¾ cup KARO® Light or Dark
    Corn Syrup
3 squares (1 ounce each)
    semisweet chocolate or
½ cup (3 ounces)
    semisweet chocolate
    chips
½ cup sugar
2 eggs, slightly beaten
1 teaspoon vanilla
1¼ cups coarsely chopped
    pecans

1. Preheat oven to 350°F. Prepare Bar Cookie Crust according to recipe directions.

2. Meanwhile, for filling, in heavy 3-quart saucepan stir corn syrup and chocolate over low heat just until chocolate melts. Remove from heat. Stir in sugar, eggs and vanilla until blended. Stir in pecans. Pour over hot crust; spread evenly.

3. Bake 20 minutes or until filling is firm around edges and slightly soft in center. Cool completely on wire rack. Cut into 2×1½-inch bars.   *Makes about 32 bars*

Coconut Pecan Bars

COCONUT PECAN BARS

1¼ cups granulated sugar, divided

½ cup plus 3 tablespoons all-purpose flour, divided

1½ cups finely chopped pecans, divided

¾ cup (1½ sticks) butter or margarine, softened, divided

2 large eggs

1 tablespoon vanilla extract

1¾ cups "M&M's"® Chocolate Mini Baking Bits, divided

1 cup shredded coconut

Preheat oven to 350°F. Lightly grease 13×9×2-inch baking pan; set aside. In large bowl combine ¾ cup sugar, ½ cup flour and ½ cup nuts; add ¼ cup melted butter and mix well. Press mixture onto bottom of prepared pan. Bake 10 minutes or until set; cool slightly. In large bowl cream remaining ½ cup butter and ½ cup sugar; beat in eggs and vanilla. Combine 1 cup "M&M's"® Chocolate Mini Baking Bits and remaining 3 tablespoons flour; stir into creamed mixture. Spread mixture over cooled crust. Combine coconut and remaining 1 cup nuts; sprinkle over batter. Sprinkle remaining ¾ cup "M&M's"® Chocolate Mini Baking Bits over coconut and nuts; pat down lightly. Bake 25 to 30 minutes or until set. Cool completely. Cut into bars. Store in tightly covered container. *Makes 24 bars*

CHRISTMAS COOKIE HOUSE

COOKIE DOUGH:
2¾ cups flour
1 teaspoon ground ginger
½ teaspoon cinnamon
¼ teaspoon salt
⅔ cup KARO® Light Corn Syrup
½ cup packed brown sugar
6 tablespoons MAZOLA® Margarine or butter
Gingerbread House Cookie Mold*
MAZOLA NO STICK® Cooking Spray
Decorator Icing (page 285)
Assorted candy for decorations such as colored sugar crystals, spearmint leaves, various small colored candies or peppermint candies

All Occasion Gingerbread House Cookie Mold is available in Williams-Sonoma retail stores. To order, dial 1-800-541-2233.

FOR COOKIE DOUGH

In large bowl stir flour, ginger, cinnamon and salt. In 1-quart saucepan combine corn syrup, brown sugar and margarine; stir over medium heat until margarine is melted. Stir into flour mixture until well blended. On waxed paper, press dough into a rectangle; cut into three equal parts. (Do not refrigerate dough before molding.)

Preheat oven to 350°F. Spray Gingerbread House Cookie Mold with cooking spray. Firmly press one-third of dough into mold sections. Bake 25 minutes or until lightly browned. Cool 5 minutes. Carefully remove pieces from mold. Cool on wire racks. Cool cookie mold until it can be handled. Repeat to make second half of house.

On waxed paper-lined cookie sheet, roll remaining dough ⅛ inch thick. Cut into people, trees, animals or desired shapes with cookie cutters. Remove dough trimmings and reroll; arrange cookies on ungreased cookie sheets. Bake 10 to 13 minutes or until lightly browned. Remove from cookie sheets; cool on wire racks.

TO ASSEMBLE HOUSE

Cover 13-inch square of heavy cardboard with foil. In center draw 5×4½-inch rectangle to serve as guide for base of house. Fill pastry bag fitted with plain tip with Decorator Icing. On one front wall of house, pipe icing along inside of one side and along bottom edge. On one side wall of house, pipe icing along bottom edge. Following guidelines, carefully stand front and side wall pieces on cardboard base, placing edge of side wall against inside edge of front wall. Pipe extra icing on inside seams for extra strength. Front and side walls should stand alone. If necessary, hold in place a few minutes

until icing sets. Repeat with remaining back and side walls, piping icing along ends of side walls. Carefully press walls together to form the house. Let stand 10 minutes to set.

TO ATTACH ROOF

Pipe icing along top edge of front wall, and front half of side walls. Place one roof piece on top of house; hold or prop in place about 5 minutes or until set. Pipe icing along top edge of back wall and back half of side walls. Pipe icing along roof edges where roof pieces will meet. Place remaining roof section on house so that roof pieces meet to form peak; hold or prop in place about 5 minutes or until set. Use icing to fill in any spaces along peak of house. Attach chimney with icing.

Use icing to attach candies to roof and chimney. Add spearmint leaf "shrubs" to sides of house and a candy pathway. Decorate cookie trees and people with icing, colored sugars and candies. Attach to base with icing.

Makes about 2 cups

Decorator Icing: *In large bowl with mixer at low speed, beat 1 pound confectioners sugar, ½ cup warm water, 3 tablespoons meringue powder** and ½ teaspoon cream of tartar until blended. Beat at high speed 7 to 10 minutes or until knife drawn through mixture leaves a path. Divide and color as desired. Keep covered with damp cloth at all times.*

**Meringue powder is available from specialty cake decorating suppliers or by contacting Wilton Industries, 2240 West 75th Street, Woodridge, IL 60517. Phone: (630) 963-7100, ext. 320.

VISIONS OF SUGARPLUMS

Dark Chocolate Fudge

½ cup whipping cream
½ cup light corn syrup
3 cups (18 ounces) semisweet
    chocolate chips
1½ cups powdered sugar, sifted
½ cup chopped walnuts
    (optional)
1½ teaspoons vanilla extract

Line 8-inch square baking pan with foil, extending edges over sides of pan.

Bring cream and corn syrup to a boil in 2-quart saucepan over medium heat. Boil 1 minute. Remove from heat. Stir in chocolate. Cook until chocolate is melted, stirring constantly. Stir in powdered sugar, walnuts and vanilla. Pour into prepared pan. Spread mixture into corners. Cover; refrigerate 2 hours or until firm.

Lift fudge out of pan using foil; remove foil. Cut into 1-inch squares. Store in airtight container.

Makes about 2 pounds or 64 candies

Peanut Butter Fudge: *Prepare Dark Chocolate Fudge as directed, substituting 2 packages (10 ounces each) peanut butter chips for the semisweet chocolate chips.*

Makes about 2 pounds or 64 candies

Clockwise from top right: Peanut Butter Fudge, Dark Chocolate Fudge and Traditional Peanut Brittle (page 345) **287**

Fast 'n' Fabulous Chocolate Fudge

½ cup **KARO®** **Light or Dark**
   Corn Syrup
⅓ **cup evaporated milk**
 3 **cups (18 ounces) semisweet**
   chocolate chips
¾ **cup confectioners sugar,**
   sifted
 2 **teaspoons vanilla**
 1 **cup coarsely chopped nuts**
   (optional)

1. Microwave Directions: Line 8-inch square baking pan with plastic wrap.

2. In 3-quart microwavable bowl combine corn syrup and evaporated milk; stir until well blended. Microwave on HIGH (100%) 3 minutes. Stir in chocolate chips until melted.

3. Stir in confectioners sugar, vanilla and nuts. With wooden spoon, beat until thick and glossy.

4. Spread in prepared pan. Refrigerate 2 hours or until firm.
Makes 25 squares

Marvelous Marble Fudge: *Omit nuts. Prepare as directed in steps 1 through 3; spread in prepared pan. Drop ⅓ cup SKIPPY® Creamy Peanut Butter over fudge in small dollops. Swirl fudge to marbleize. Continue as directed.*

Double Peanut Butter Chocolate Fudge: *Prepare as directed in steps 1 and 2. In step 3, stir in ⅓ cup SKIPPY® SUPER CHUNK® Peanut Butter. Spread in prepared pan. Drop additional ⅓ cup peanut butter over fudge in small dollops. With small spatula, swirl fudge to marbleize. Continue as directed.*

Fast 'n' Fabulous Chocolate Fudge

TRIPLE LAYER CHOCOLATE MINTS

6 ounces semisweet
  chocolate, chopped
6 ounces white chocolate,
  chopped
1 teaspoon peppermint
  extract
6 ounces milk chocolate,
  chopped

1. Line 8-inch square pan with foil, leaving 1-inch overhang on sides. Place semisweet chocolate in top of double boiler over simmering water. Stir until melted. Remove from heat.

2. Spread melted chocolate onto bottom of prepared pan. Let stand until firm. (If not firm after 45 minutes, refrigerate 10 minutes.)

3. Melt white chocolate in clean double boiler; stir in peppermint extract. Spread over semisweet chocolate layer. Shake pan to spread evenly. Let stand 45 minutes or until set.

4. Melt milk chocolate in same double boiler. Spread over white chocolate layer. Shake pan to spread evenly. Let stand 45 minutes or until set.

5. Cut mints into 16 (2-inch) squares. Remove from pan by lifting mints and foil with foil handles. Cut each square diagonally into 2 triangles. Cut in half again to make 64 small triangles. Store in airtight container in refrigerator.

Makes 64 mints

COCONUT FUDGE

2 packages (3 ounces each)
  cream cheese, softened
4½ to 5¼ cups powdered sugar
1 cup chopped blanched
  almonds
1 cup flaked coconut
½ teaspoon coconut extract
  Sliced almonds (optional)

1. Butter 8-inch square pan; set aside. Beat cream cheese and enough powdered sugar in a medium bowl with electric mixer to make a stiff, but not dry mixture.

2. Stir in chopped almonds, coconut and coconut extract. Press mixture into prepared pan. Arrange sliced almonds on top; gently press into fudge. Score fudge into squares with knife. Refrigerate until firm. Cut into squares. Store in refrigerator.

Makes about 2 pounds

Triple Layer Chocolate Mints

Chocolate-Nut Squares

1 cup (6 ounces) semisweet chocolate chips
1 cup milk chocolate chips
1 tablespoon shortening
1 package (14 ounces) caramels
2 tablespoons butter
3 tablespoons milk
2 cups coarsely chopped pecans

Line 8-inch square pan with buttered foil; set aside. Melt chips with shortening in small saucepan over very low heat, stirring constantly. Spoon half the chocolate mixture into prepared pan, spreading evenly over bottom and ¼ inch up sides of pan. Refrigerate until firm.

Meanwhile, combine caramels, butter and milk in medium saucepan. Cook over medium heat, stirring constantly. When mixture is smooth, stir in pecans. Cool to lukewarm. Spread caramel mixture evenly over chocolate in pan. Melt remaining chocolate mixture again over very low heat, stirring constantly; spread over caramel layer. Refrigerate until almost firm. Cut into squares. Store in refrigerator.

Makes about 2 pounds

Note: Squares are easier to cut without breaking if chocolate is not completely firm.

Chocolate Peppermints

1 cup (6 ounces) semisweet chocolate chips
1 cup milk chocolate chips
¼ teaspoon peppermint extract
½ cup crushed peppermint candy

Line baking sheet with buttered waxed paper; set aside. Melt chips in medium saucepan over low heat, stirring constantly. Stir in peppermint extract. Spread mixture in rectangle about ¼ inch thick on prepared baking sheet. Sprinkle with candy; press into chocolate. Refrigerate until almost firm. Cut into squares. Refrigerate until firm before removing from paper.

Makes about 100 mints

Hint: Squares are easier to cut without breaking if chocolate is not completely firm.

Chocolate-Nut Squares and Chocolate Peppermints

293

Rich Cocoa Fudge

3 cups sugar
⅔ cup HERSHEY'S Cocoa or HERSHEY'S European Style Cocoa
⅛ teaspoon salt
1½ cups milk
¼ cup (½ stick) butter or margarine
1 teaspoon vanilla extract

Line 8- or 9-inch square pan with foil, extending foil over edges of pan. Butter foil. In heavy 4-quart saucepan, stir together sugar, cocoa and salt; stir in milk. Cook over medium heat, stirring constantly, until mixture comes to a full rolling boil. Boil, without stirring, until mixture reaches 234°F on candy thermometer or until small amount of mixture dropped into very cold water, forms a soft ball which flattens when removed from water. (Bulb of thermometer should not rest on bottom of saucepan.) Remove from heat. Add butter and vanilla. (Do not stir.) Cool at room temperature to 110°F (lukewarm). Beat with wooden spoon until fudge thickens and just begins to lose some of its gloss. Quickly spread into prepared pan; cool completely. Use foil to lift fudge out of pan; peel off foil. Cut into squares. Store in tightly covered container at room temperature.

Makes about 3 dozen pieces or 1¾ pounds fudge

Nutty Rich Cocoa Fudge: *Beat cooked fudge as directed. Immediately stir in 1 cup chopped almonds, pecans or walnuts; quickly spread into prepared pan.*

Marshmallow-Nut Cocoa Fudge: *Increase cocoa to ¾ cup. Cook fudge as directed. Add 1 cup marshmallow creme with butter and vanilla. (Do not stir.) Cool to 110°F (lukewarm). Beat 10 minutes; stir in 1 cup chopped nuts. Pour into prepared pan. (Fudge does not set until poured into pan.) For best results, do not double this recipe.*

Left to right: Nutty Rich Cocoa Fudge and Double-Decker Fudge (page 296)

DOUBLE-DECKER FUDGE

1 cup REESE'S® Peanut Butter Chips
1 cup HERSHEY'S Semi-Sweet Chocolate Chips or HERSHEY'S MINI CHIPS™ Semi-Sweet Chocolate
2¼ cups sugar
1 jar (7 ounces) marshmallow creme
¾ cup evaporated milk
¼ cup (½ stick) butter or margarine
1 teaspoon vanilla extract

Line 8-inch square pan with foil, extending foil over edges of pan. In medium bowl, place peanut butter chips. In second medium bowl, place chocolate chips. In heavy 3-quart saucepan, combine sugar, marshmallow creme, evaporated milk and butter. Cook over medium heat, stirring constantly, until mixture comes to a boil; boil 5 minutes, stirring constantly. Remove from heat; stir in vanilla. Immediately stir half of the hot mixture (1½ cups) into peanut butter chips until chips are completely melted; quickly spread into prepared pan. Stir remaining hot mixture into chocolate chips until chips are completely melted. Quickly spread over top of peanut butter layer. Cool to room temperature; refrigerate until firm. Use foil to lift fudge out of pan; peel off foil. Cut into 1-inch squares. Store in tightly covered container at room temperature.

Makes about 5 dozen pieces or about 2 pounds fudge

Peanut Butter Fudge: *Omit chocolate chips; place 1⅔ cups (10-ounce package) REESE'S® Peanut Butter Chips in large bowl. Cook fudge mixture as directed. Add to chips; stir until chips are completely melted. Pour into prepared pan; cool to room temperature.*

Chocolate Fudge: *Omit peanut butter chips; place 2 cups (12-ounce package) HERSHEY'S Semi-Sweet Chocolate Chips or HERSHEY'S MINI CHIPS™ Semi-Sweet Chocolate in large bowl. Cook fudge mixture as directed. Add to chips; stir until chips are completely melted. Pour into prepared pan; cool to room temperature.*

CHOCOLATE MINT SQUARES

6 tablespoons butter (do not use margarine)
½ cup HERSHEY'S Cocoa
2 cups powdered sugar
3 tablespoons plus
   1 teaspoon milk, divided
1 teaspoon vanilla extract
   Mint Filling (recipe follows)

Line 8-inch square pan with foil, extending foil over edges of pan. In small saucepan over low heat, melt butter; add cocoa. Cook, stirring constantly, just until mixture is smooth. Remove from heat; add powdered sugar, 3 tablespoons milk and vanilla. Cook over low heat, stirring constantly, until mixture is glossy. Spread half of mixture into prepared pan. Refrigerate. Meanwhile, prepare Mint Filling; spread filling over chocolate layer. Refrigerate 10 minutes. To remaining chocolate mixture in saucepan, add remaining 1 teaspoon milk. Cook over low heat, stirring constantly, until smooth. Spread quickly over filling. Refrigerate until firm. Use foil to lift candy out of pan; peel off foil. Cut candy into squares. Store in tightly covered container in refrigerator.

Makes about 4 dozen pieces

MINT FILLING

1 package (3 ounces) cream cheese, softened
2 cups powdered sugar
½ teaspoon vanilla extract
¼ teaspoon peppermint extract
3 to 5 drops green food color
Milk

In small mixer bowl, beat cream cheese, powdered sugar, vanilla, peppermint extract and food color until smooth. Add 2 to 3 teaspoons milk, if needed, for spreading consistency.

Mocha Marshmallow Fudge

1 tablespoon instant coffee
1 tablespoon boiling water
2½ cups sugar
½ cup butter
1 can (5 ounces) evaporated milk
1½ cups semisweet chocolate chips
1 jar (7 ounces) marshmallow creme
½ teaspoon vanilla

Line 9-inch square baking pan with foil, extending edges over sides of pan. Lightly grease foil with butter. Dissolve coffee in water; set aside.

Place sugar, butter and evaporated milk in medium saucepan; bring to a boil over medium-high heat, stirring constantly. Reduce heat to medium. Continue boiling 5 minutes, stirring constantly. Remove from heat. Immediately stir in reserved coffee mixture, chocolate, marshmallow creme and vanilla. Pour into prepared pan. Let stand 1 hour.

Lift candy out of pan using foil; remove foil. Cut into 1-inch squares. Cover; refrigerate until fudge is set.

Makes about 2½ pounds or 64 pieces

Peanut Butter Fudge

1 (16-ounce) box DOMINO® Light Brown Sugar (approximately 2¼ cups)
½ cup milk
2 tablespoons butter
¾ cup peanut butter
1 teaspoon vanilla
½ cup chopped peanuts

Butter a 9×5-inch loaf pan; set aside. Heat sugar, milk and butter in a heavy 2-quart saucepan. Bring to a boil, stirring constantly until the sugar is dissolved. Continue boiling 5 minutes longer, stirring constantly. Cool 10 minutes. Add peanut butter, vanilla and peanuts. Stir until well blended. Pour into prepared pan. Refrigerate at least 3 hours.

Makes about 27 candies

Top to bottom: Mocha Marshmallow Fudge and Chocolate Butter Crunch (page 340)

299

EASY TURTLE FUDGE

1 package (12 ounces)
   semisweet chocolate
   chips
2 ounces bittersweet or
   semisweet chocolate,
   chopped
1 cup sweetened condensed
   milk
¼ teaspoon salt
30 individually wrapped
   caramel candies,
   unwrapped
1 tablespoon water
40 pecan halves

1. Grease 11×7-inch pan; set aside.

2. Melt chips in medium saucepan over low heat, stirring constantly. Stir in bittersweet chocolate until melted. Stir in sweetened condensed milk and salt until smooth. Spread evenly in prepared pan; cover with foil. Refrigerate until firm.

3. Cut fudge into 40 squares. Transfer to baking sheet lined with waxed paper, placing squares ½ inch apart.

4. Place caramels and water in small saucepan. Heat over low heat until melted, stirring frequently. Drizzle or top fudge pieces with caramel mixture. Top each piece with 1 pecan half. Store in airtight container in refrigerator.

Makes 40 candies

CHERRY VANILLA FUDGE

MAZOLA NO STICK®
   Cooking Spray
2 cups sugar
½ cup sour cream
⅓ cup KARO® Light or Dark
   Corn Syrup
2 tablespoons MAZOLA®
   Margarine or butter
¼ teaspoon salt
1 cup coarsely chopped
   walnuts
½ cup coarsely chopped dried
   cherries or cranberries
2 teaspoons vanilla

1. Spray 8- or 9-inch square baking pan with cooking spray. In 3-quart saucepan combine sugar, sour cream, corn syrup, margarine and salt. Stirring constantly, bring to boil over medium heat and boil 5 minutes. Remove from heat. Without stirring, let stand 15 minutes. Stir in walnuts, cherries and vanilla. Quickly spread in prepared pan. Refrigerate 2 hours or until firm. Cut into squares.   *Makes about 36 squares*

Easy Turtle Fudge

BUTTERSCOTCH ROCKY ROAD

1½ cups miniature
marshmallows
1 cup coarsely chopped
pecans
2 cups (12 ounces)
butterscotch chips
½ cup sweetened condensed
milk

1. Butter 13×9-inch pan. Spread marshmallows and pecans evenly on bottom of pan.

2. Melt butterscotch chips in medium saucepan over low heat, stirring constantly. Stir in condensed milk.

3. Pour butterscotch mixture over marshmallows and pecans, covering entire mixture. If necessary, use a knife or small spatula to help cover the marshmallows and nuts with butterscotch mixture. Let stand in pan until set. Cut into squares. Store in refrigerator.   *Makes about 1 pound*

LAYERED FUDGE

1 cup (6 ounces) semisweet
chocolate chips
1 can (14 ounces) sweetened
condensed milk, divided
1 teaspoon vanilla
1 cup miniature
marshmallows
2 cups (12 ounces)
butterscotch chips
½ cup chopped pecans

1. Butter 8-inch square pan; set aside. Melt chocolate chips in small saucepan over very low heat, stirring constantly. Remove from heat. Stir in ¾ cup condensed milk and vanilla until smooth. Stir in marshmallows; pour into prepared pan. Refrigerate until firm.

2. Meanwhile, melt butterscotch chips in small saucepan over very low heat, stirring constantly. Remove from heat; stir in remaining condensed milk until smooth. Stir in pecans.

3. Cool mixture to room temperature; spoon over chocolate layer. Score fudge into squares with knife. Refrigerate until firm. Cut into squares. Store in refrigerator.

Makes about 2 pounds

Hint: For a different look, prepare butterscotch layer first, then top with chocolate layer.

Left to right: Peanut Butter Cups (page 354) and Butterscotch Rocky Road

Penuche

1 cup half-and-half
2 tablespoons butter
2 cups packed brown sugar
1 cup granulated sugar
2 teaspoons vanilla
1 cup chopped pecans

1. Butter 8-inch square pan; set aside. Combine half-and-half, butter, brown sugar and granulated sugar in medium saucepan. Cook over medium heat, stirring constantly, until sugar dissolves and mixture comes to a boil.

2. Add candy thermometer. (Bulb of thermometer should not rest on bottom of saucepan.) Continue to cook until mixture reaches the soft-ball stage (238°F). Pour into large heat-proof mixer bowl. Cool to lukewarm (about 110°F).

3. Add vanilla and beat with electric mixer until thick. Beat in pecans when candy loses its gloss. Spread into prepared pan. Score fudge into squares with knife. Refrigerate until firm. Cut into squares. Store in refrigerator.

Makes about 1 pound

Eggnog Fudge

2 cups sugar
¾ cup eggnog
2 tablespoons corn syrup
2 tablespoons butter
1 teaspoon vanilla

1. Butter 8-inch square pan; set aside. Combine sugar, eggnog, corn syrup and butter in medium saucepan. Cook over medium heat, stirring constantly, until sugar dissolves and mixture comes to a boil.

2. Add candy thermometer. (Bulb of thermometer should not rest on bottom of saucepan.) Continue to cook until mixture reaches the soft-ball stage (238°F). Pour into large heat-proof mixer bowl. Cool to lukewarm (about 110°F).

3. Add vanilla and beat with electric mixer until thick. Spread into prepared pan. Score fudge into squares with knife. Refrigerate until firm. Cut into squares. Store in refrigerator.

Makes about 1 pound

Penuche

305

CHOCOLATE CHIP COOKIE DOUGH FUDGE

⅓ cup butter, melted
⅓ cup packed brown sugar
¾ cup all-purpose flour
½ teaspoon salt, divided
1⅓ cups mini semisweet
    chocolate chips, divided
1 package (1 pound)
    powdered sugar
1 package (8 ounces) cream
    cheese, softened
1 teaspoon vanilla

Make this fudge for the cookie dough lovers in your life. The combination of chocolate chip cookie dough and chocolate fudge will be a hit; and, it is safe to eat the cookie dough because it does not contain raw eggs.

1. Line 8- or 9-inch square pan with foil, leaving 1-inch overhang on sides. Lightly butter foil.

2. Combine butter and brown sugar in small bowl. Stir in flour and ¼ teaspoon salt. Stir in ⅓ cup chips. Form dough into a ball. Place on plastic wrap; flatten into a disc. Wrap disc in plastic wrap; freeze 10 minutes or until firm.

3. Unwrap dough; cut into ½-inch pieces; refrigerate.

4. Place powdered sugar, cream cheese, vanilla and remaining ¼ teaspoon salt in large bowl. Beat with electric mixer at low speed until combined. Scrape down side of bowl; beat at medium speed until smooth.

5. Melt remaining 1 cup chips in heavy small saucepan over very low heat, stirring constantly.

6. Add melted chocolate to cream cheese mixture; beat just until blended. Stir in chilled cookie dough pieces. Spread evenly in prepared pan.

7. Refrigerate until firm. Remove from pan by lifting fudge and foil using foil handles. Cut into squares. Store in airtight container in refrigerator.

Makes about 3 to 4 dozen candies

Chocolate Chip Cookie Dough Fudge

COCONUT-ALMOND BARS

2 cups powdered sugar, sifted
1 cup coconut
⅓ cup plus 1 tablespoon sweetened condensed milk
1 teaspoon vanilla
½ cup milk chocolate chips
½ cup semisweet chocolate chips
1 tablespoon shortening
1 cup blanched whole almonds

1. Line 8-inch square pan with buttered foil. Set aside.

2. Combine sugar, coconut, condensed milk and vanilla in medium bowl. Press into prepared pan. Refrigerate until firm.

3. Melt chips with shortening in small saucepan over low heat, stirring constantly.

4. Spread evenly over coconut mixture in pan. Press almonds into chocolate in rows 1 inch apart. Score into 2×1-inch bars. Refrigerate until almost firm. Cut into bars. Store in refrigerator. *Makes 32 bars*

BUTTERMILK FUDGE

1 cup buttermilk
1 teaspoon baking soda
2 cups sugar
2 tablespoons corn syrup
2 tablespoons butter
1 teaspoon vanilla
1 cup chopped pecans

1. Butter 8-inch square pan; set aside. Combine buttermilk and baking soda in 3-quart saucepan; then add sugar, corn syrup and butter. Cook over medium heat, stirring constantly, until sugar dissolves and mixture comes to a boil.

2. Add candy thermometer; reduce heat to low. (Bulb of thermometer should not rest on bottom of saucepan.) Stir mixture occasionally. Continue to cook until mixture reaches the soft-ball stage (238°F). Pour into large heat-proof mixer bowl. Cool to lukewarm (about 110°F).

3. Add vanilla and beat with electric mixer until thick. Beat in pecans when candy starts to lose its gloss. Spread in prepared pan. Score fudge into squares with knife. Refrigerate until firm. Cut into squares. Store in refrigerator. *Makes about 1 pound*

Top to bottom: Raisin Clusters (page 347), Cherry-Chocolate Logs (page 368), Chocolate Fudge-Peanut Butter Balls (page 336) and Coconut-Almond Bars

Classic Coconut Bonbons

2 packages (1 pound each)
    powdered sugar, divided
1 can (14 ounces) sweetened
    condensed milk
½ cup butter
2 teaspoons vanilla
2 cups flaked coconut
1 cup finely chopped pecans
2 pounds premium
    bittersweet chocolate

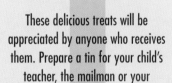

These delicious treats will be appreciated by anyone who receives them. Prepare a tin for your child's teacher, the mailman or your neighbors.

1. Sift ½ of powdered sugar into large bowl with fine-meshed sieve or sifter; set aside.

2. Place sweetened condensed milk and butter in small saucepan; cook over low heat until butter melts and mixture is blended, stirring frequently. Remove from heat; stir in vanilla.

3. Pour hot butter mixture over reserved powdered sugar; beat with electric mixer at medium speed until blended. Sift remaining powdered sugar into bowl; continue to beat until blended and creamy. Stir in coconut and pecans with wooden spoon until combined. Cover with plastic wrap; refrigerate 1 hour.

4. Shape coconut mixture into 1-inch balls. Place on baking sheet lined with waxed paper. Refrigerate until firm.

5. Temper chocolate. (See page 7.)

6. Dip balls in tempered chocolate with dipping fork or spoon, tapping handle against side of pan to allow excess chocolate to drain back into pan.

7. Remove excess chocolate by scraping bottom of bonbon across rim of saucepan.

8. Place bonbons on waxed paper; sign bonbons, if desired. Let stand in cool place until chocolate is firm. (Do not refrigerate.) Store in airtight container at room temperature.
Makes about 10 dozen bonbons (4½ pounds)

Classic Coconut Bonbons

TROPICAL SUGARPLUMS

½ cup white chocolate chips
¼ cup light corn syrup
½ cup chopped dates
¼ cup chopped maraschino
 cherries, well drained
1 teaspoon vanilla
¼ teaspoon rum extract
1¼ cups crushed gingersnaps
 Flaked coconut

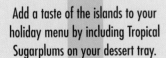

Add a taste of the islands to your holiday menu by including Tropical Sugarplums on your dessert tray.

1. Combine chips and corn syrup in large skillet. Cook and stir over low heat until melted and smooth.

2. Stir in dates, cherries, vanilla and rum extract until well blended. Add gingersnaps, stirring until well blended. (Mixture will be stiff.)

3. Form mixture into ¾-inch balls; roll in coconut. Place in small foil cups, if desired. Serve immediately or let stand overnight to allow flavors to blend.

Makes about 2 dozen cookies

Tropical Sugarplums

Eggnog Truffles

2 cups (11½ ounces) milk chocolate chips
½ cup eggnog
2 tablespoons butter
36 chocolate cups, either purchased or homemade (recipe follows)

1. Melt chips with eggnog and butter in medium saucepan over low heat, stirring occasionally. Pour into pie pan. Refrigerate until mixture is thick, but soft, about 2 hours.

2. Spoon truffle mixture into pastry bag fitted with large star tip. Pipe mixture into chocolate cups. Truffles can be refrigerated 2 to 3 days or frozen several weeks.

Makes about 36 truffles

Chocolate Cups

2 cups (12 ounces) semisweet chocolate chips
1 tablespoon shortening

1. Melt chips with shortening in small saucepan over very low heat, stirring constantly.

2. Spoon about ½ tablespoonful of the chocolate mixture into each of about 36 small foil candy cups. With back of spoon, bring some of the chocolate up side of each cup. Refrigerate until firm.

Makes about 36 cups

Hint: To remove foil cups, cut slit in bottom of cup and peel foil up from bottom. Do not peel down from top edge.

Top to bottom: White Chocolate Truffles (page 316), Easy Orange Truffles (page 316) and Eggnog Truffles

WHITE CHOCOLATE TRUFFLES

12 ounces white chocolate, coarsely chopped
⅓ cup whipping cream
2 tablespoons orange liqueur
1 teaspoon grated orange zest
1 to 1¼ cups powdered sugar

1. Melt white chocolate with whipping cream in medium saucepan over low heat, stirring constantly. Whisk in liqueur and zest until blended. Pour into pie pan. Refrigerate until mixture is fudgy, but soft, about 2 hours.

2. Shape about 1 tablespoonful of the mixture into 1¼-inch ball. Repeat with remaining mixture. Place balls on waxed paper.

3. Sift sugar into shallow bowl. Roll balls in sugar; place in small candy cups. Truffles can be refrigerated 2 to 3 days or frozen several weeks. *Makes about 36 truffles*

EASY ORANGE TRUFFLES

1 cup (6 ounces) semisweet chocolate chips
2 squares (1 ounce each) unsweetened chocolate, chopped
1½ cups powdered sugar
½ cup butter, softened
1 tablespoon grated orange peel
1 tablespoon orange-flavored liqueur
2 squares (1 ounce each) semisweet chocolate, grated or cocoa

Melt chocolate chips and unsweetened chocolate in small saucepan over very low heat, stirring constantly; set aside.

Combine powdered sugar, butter, orange peel and liqueur in small bowl. Beat with electric mixer until combined. Beat in cooled chocolate. Pour into pie pan. Refrigerate about 30 minutes or until mixture is fudgy and can be shaped into balls.

Shape scant 1 tablespoonful of mixture into 1-inch ball. Repeat with remaining mixture. Place balls on waxed paper.

Sprinkle grated chocolate or cocoa in shallow bowl. Roll balls in grated chocolate or cocoa; place in small candy cups. (If coating mixture won't stick because truffle has set, roll between your palms until outside is soft.) Store in airtight container up to 3 days in refrigerator or several weeks in freezer. *Makes about 34 truffles*

CREAM TRUFFLES

2 cups (12 ounces) semisweet chocolate chips
¼ cup whipping cream
¼ cup butter
3 tablespoons cream liqueur
½ to ¾ cup powdered sugar

1. Melt chips with whipping cream and butter in medium saucepan over low heat, stirring occasionally. Stir in liqueur. Pour into pie pan. Refrigerate until mixture is fudgy, but soft, about 2 hours.

2. Shape about 1 tablespoonful of the mixture into 1¼-inch ball. Repeat with remaining mixture. Place balls on waxed paper.

3. Sift sugar into shallow bowl. Roll balls in sugar; place in small candy cups. (If coating mixture won't stick because truffle has set, roll between palms until outside is soft.) Truffles can be refrigerated 2 to 3 days or frozen several weeks.

Makes about 36 truffles

EASY CHOCOLATE TRUFFLES

1 package (8 ounces) PHILADELPHIA BRAND® Cream Cheese, softened
3 cups powdered sugar
1½ packages (12 ounces) BAKER'S® Semi-Sweet Chocolate, melted
1½ teaspoons vanilla
Ground nuts, unsweetened cocoa or BAKER'S® ANGEL FLAKE® Coconut, toasted

BEAT cream cheese until smooth. Gradually add sugar, beating until well blended. Add melted chocolate and vanilla; mix well. Refrigerate about 1 hour. Shape into 1-inch balls. Roll in nuts, cocoa or coconut. Store in refrigerator.

Makes about 5 dozen candies

Tip: To flavor truffles with liqueurs, omit vanilla. Divide truffle mixture into thirds. Add 1 tablespoon liqueur (almond, coffee or orange) to each third mixture; mix well.

Cookies and Cream Cheesecake Bonbons

COOKIES AND CREAM CHEESECAKE BONBONS

24 chocolate cream-filled cookies, divided
1 package (8 ounces) cream cheese, softened
1 cup nonfat dry milk
1 teaspoon vanilla
1 package (1 pound) powdered sugar

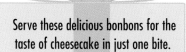

Serve these delicious bonbons for the taste of cheesecake in just one bite.

1. Coarsely chop 12 cookies; set aside.

2. Place remaining 12 cookies in food processor; process until fine crumbs form. Place crumbs on baking sheet lined with waxed paper; set aside.

3. Beat cream cheese, dry milk and vanilla in medium bowl with electric mixer at medium speed until smooth. Beat in powdered sugar, 1 cup at a time, at low speed until mixture is smooth. Stir in reserved chopped cookies. Refrigerate 2 hours or until firm.

4. Shape rounded tablespoonfuls cream cheese mixture into balls. Roll balls in reserved cookie crumbs. Store in airtight container in refrigerator.   *Makes about 3 dozen bonbons*

PEANUT BUTTER CONFECTIONS

1½ cups nonfat dry milk
1 cup creamy peanut butter
1 cup honey
1 cup flaked coconut
1 cup graham cracker crumbs
or 1 cup flaked coconut

1. Line baking sheet with waxed paper; set aside.

2. Combine milk, peanut butter, honey and 1 cup coconut in medium bowl. Refrigerate until firm enough to shape into balls, about 30 minutes.

3. Shape peanut butter mixture into 1-inch balls.

4. Place crumbs in shallow bowl. Roll balls in crumbs. Place balls on prepared baking sheet. Refrigerate until set. Store in refrigerator in airtight container.   *Makes about 48 balls*

RASPBERRY TRUFFLES

2 cups (12 ounces) semisweet
     chocolate chips
¾ cup sweetened condensed
     milk
¼ cup seedless raspberry jam
2 tablespoons butter
1 tablespoon framboise
     (raspberry brandy)
3 ounces white chocolate,
     coarsely chopped

1. Melt chips with condensed milk, jam and butter in heavy, medium saucepan over low heat, stirring occasionally. Whisk in brandy until blended. Pour into pie pan. Refrigerate until mixture is fudgy, but soft, about 1½ hours.

2. Melt white chocolate in top of double boiler over hot, not boiling water, stirring constantly; set aside.

3. Shape about 1 tablespoonful of the mixture into 1¼-inch ball. Repeat with remaining mixture. Place balls on waxed paper.

4. Spoon melted white chocolate over top one third of each truffle. Refrigerate until chocolate is firm.

5. Remove from waxed paper; place in small candy cups. Truffles can be refrigerated 2 to 3 days or frozen several weeks.   *Makes about 40 truffles*

Clockwise from top: Peanut Butter Confections, Toasted Almond Bark (page 351) and Chocolate-Granola Bars (page 350) **321**

COCONUT BALLS

½ cup golden raisins, chopped
½ cup pitted prunes or dates, chopped
½ cup graham cracker crumbs
½ cup powdered sugar
1 tablespoon grated orange peel
½ cup sweetened condensed milk
1 cup shredded coconut

1. Combine raisins, prunes, crumbs, sugar and peel in medium bowl. Stir in condensed milk. Refrigerate until firm enough to shape into balls, about 30 minutes.

2. Place coconut in shallow bowl.

3. Shape mixture into 1-inch balls. Roll in coconut. Store in refrigerator in airtight container. *Makes about 30 balls*

BOURBON BALLS

1 cup powdered sugar
2 tablespoons unsweetened cocoa powder
2 cups finely crushed vanilla wafers (about 44 wafers)
1 cup finely chopped walnuts
¼ cup bourbon
3 tablespoons corn syrup
Additional sifted powdered sugar for rolling

1. Sift 1 cup powdered sugar and cocoa into medium bowl. Add crushed vanilla wafers and walnuts. Stir bourbon and corn syrup into crumb mixture. Refrigerate until firm enough to shape into balls, about 30 minutes.

2. Shape bourbon mixture into 1-inch balls. Store in refrigerator in airtight container for 2 to 3 days. Before serving, roll in additional powdered sugar.

Makes 30 balls

Coconut Balls

CHOCOLATE-DIPPED PEANUT BUTTER CANDIES

Dipping Chocolate (recipe follows)
½ cup creamy peanut butter
6 tablespoons butter, softened
1 tablespoon light corn syrup
1 teaspoon vanilla extract
2 cups powdered sugar
1 cup graham cracker crumbs

For extra decoration and crunch, sprinkle chopped peanuts on these candies before the chocolate sets.

Line large cookie sheet with waxed paper. Prepare Dipping Chocolate; keep warm.

Beat peanut butter, butter, corn syrup and vanilla in large bowl with electric mixer on medium speed until smooth. Beat in powdered sugar and graham cracker crumbs on low speed until well mixed. (Mixture will look dry.)

Shape peanut butter mixture into 1-inch balls. Place on prepared cookie sheet. Dip one ball into Dipping Chocolate. Lift coated ball out of chocolate with fork, tapping fork on side of cup to remove excess chocolate. Place on prepared cookie sheet. Repeat with remaining balls. Let chocolate set completely before storing in airtight container.

Makes about 2½ dozen candies

DIPPING CHOCOLATE:

Place 1 cup (6 ounces) semisweet chocolate chips and 2 tablespoons vegetable shortening in microwavable bowl. Microwave on HIGH (100%) about 2 minutes or until melted, stirring after 1½ minutes.

Kahlua® Bonbons

¼ cup **KAHLUA**®

**4 teaspoons instant coffee
powder**

**¾ cup unsalted butter,
softened**

**1 ounce cream cheese,
softened**

2 egg yolks

1½ cups powdered sugar

**12 ounces semisweet
chocolate, chopped**

¼ cup vegetable shortening

**10 ounces amaretti cookies*,
crushed**

**Amaretti are Italian meringue
cookies and can be purchased at
Italian.or specialty food shops. If
desired, substitute an equal
amount of finely chopped toasted
hazelnuts or almonds.*

In small bowl combine KAHLUA® and coffee powder. Let stand 10 minutes. In medium bowl, cream butter with cream cheese until fluffy. Add egg yolks and sugar and beat until smooth. Stir KAHLUA® and coffee powder until powder is completely dissolved. Gradually beat into butter mixture. Drop mixture by rounded teaspoonfuls onto baking sheets or trays lined with waxed paper or plastic wrap. Set in freezer 1 hour or overnight.

When ready to dip, remove from freezer 1 sheet at a time; roll between palms to shape into balls. Return to freezer.

Melt chocolate and shortening in top of double boiler over simmering water, stirring frequently. Cool to lukewarm, stirring occasionally. Place crushed amaretti in bowl.

Using wooden skewer or toothpick, dip bonbon balls, 1 at a time, into warm chocolate. Allow excess chocolate to drip off, then transfer to bowl of amaretti crumbs. Using small spoon, sprinkle crumbs over bonbon to cover completely. Transfer to baking sheets or trays lined with clean plastic wrap. Using second skewer, gently push bonbon off dipping skewer. If hole remains, cover with additional amaretti crumbs. If chocolate becomes too thick, reheat gently as needed. Store bonbons in refrigerator.   *Makes about 4 dozen*

BLACK RUSSIAN TRUFFLES

**8 ounces premium
bittersweet chocolate,
broken into 2-inch pieces
¼ cup whipping cream
2 tablespoons butter
3½ tablespoons coffee-flavored
liqueur
1½ tablespoons vodka
1 cup chopped toasted
walnuts**

1. Place chocolate in food processor; process until chocolate is chopped.

2. Combine cream and butter in 1-cup glass measuring cup. Microwave at HIGH 1½ minutes or until butter is melted and cream begins to boil.

3. With food processor running, pour hot cream mixture through food tube; process until chocolate melts.

4. Add liqueur and vodka; process until blended. Pour chocolate mixture into medium bowl; cover with plastic wrap and refrigerate overnight.

5. Shape chocolate mixture into 1-inch balls. Roll in walnuts.

6. Store in airtight container in refrigerator. Let stand at room temperature 2 to 3 hours before serving.

Makes about 2½ dozen truffles

Brandy Truffles: Add 3½ tablespoons brandy to chocolate mixture in Step 4 in place of coffee-flavored liqueur and vodka. Roll truffles in 1 cup powdered sugar in place of walnuts.

Hazelnut Truffles: Add 3½ tablespoons hazelnut-flavored liqueur and 1½ tablespoons gold tequila to chocolate mixture in Step 4 in place of coffee-flavored liqueur and vodka. Roll truffles in 1 cup chopped toasted hazelnuts in place of walnuts.

Black Russian Truffles, Brandy Truffles and Hazelnut Truffles

327

JOLLY BOURBON BALLS

1 package (12 ounces) vanilla
    wafers, finely crushed
    (3 cups)
1 cup finely chopped nuts
1 cup powdered sugar,
    divided
1 cup (6 ounces) semisweet
    chocolate chips
½ cup light corn syrup
⅓ cup bourbon or rum

1. Combine crushed wafers, nuts and ½ cup powdered sugar in large bowl; set aside.

2. Melt chocolate with corn syrup in top of double boiler over simmering (not boiling) water. Stir in bourbon until smooth. Pour chocolate mixture over crumb mixture; stir to combine thoroughly. Shape scant 1 tablespoonful of mixture into 1-inch ball. Repeat with remaining mixture. Place on waxed paper.

3. Place remaining ½ cup powdered sugar in shallow bowl. Roll balls in powdered sugar; place in small candy cups. Store in airtight containers at least 3 days before serving for flavors to mellow. (May be stored up to 2 weeks.)

Makes about 48 candies

MERRI-MINT TRUFFLES

1 package (10 ounces) mint
    chocolate chips
⅓ cup whipping cream
¼ cup butter
1 container (3½ ounces)
    chocolate sprinkles

1. Melt chocolate chips with cream and butter in medium saucepan over low heat, stirring occasionally. Pour into pie pan. Refrigerate about 2 hours or until mixture is fudgy, but soft.

2. Shape about 1 tablespoonful of mixture into 1¼-inch ball. Repeat with remaining mixture. Place on waxed paper.

3. Place sprinkles in shallow bowl. Roll balls in sprinkles; place in small candy cups. (If coating mixture won't stick because truffle has set, roll between your palms until outside is soft.) Store in airtight container up to 3 days in refrigerator or several weeks in freezer. *Makes about 24 truffles*

Merri-Mint Truffles, Jolly Bourbon Balls and Easy Orange Truffles (page 316)

DOUBLE-CHOCOLATE COFFEE BALLS

1 can (8 ounces) almond
    paste
3 tablespoons bourbon
1 egg white
3 cups powdered sugar,
    divided
54 to 56 purchased chocolate-
    coated coffee beans
16 ounces premium semisweet
    or bittersweet chocolate,
    chopped
⅔ cup heavy cream

1. Beat almond paste, bourbon and egg white in medium bowl with electric mixer at medium speed until blended. Add 2 cups powdered sugar; beat at low speed until well mixed. Place on surface dusted with powdered sugar. Knead in remaining 1 cup powdered sugar until smooth. Shape into two 1¼-inch diameter logs. Cut one ¼-inch slice from log. Flatten slightly into a circle. Sprinkle work surface with powdered sugar as needed to prevent sticking. Keep logs covered with plastic wrap until ready to cut.

2. Place coffee bean in center of slice; fold sides up around coffee bean. With fingertips, smooth into ball. Set on tray lined with waxed paper. Cover lightly with plastic wrap. Repeat steps with remaining logs until all the balls are made. Place in freezer.

3. Melt chocolate in top of double boiler over just simmering water. Stir until chocolate is melted. While chocolate is melting, bring heavy cream to a boil over medium-high heat in small saucepan. Remove from heat. Add hot cream all at once to melted chocolate; whisk quickly until mixture is smooth and glossy (the initial graininess will disperse). Check temperature of chocolate with candy thermometer and maintain between 125° to 130°F while dipping.

4. Remove tray from freezer. Dip balls into melted chocolate with dipping fork or spoon, tapping handle a few times against side of pan to allow excess chocolate to drain back into pan. Place balls back on waxed paper. Let stand in cool place 20 minutes; refrigerate 1 hour. Place balls in foil cups. Store in airtight container in refrigerator.

Makes about 4½ dozen balls

Double-Chocolate Coffee Balls

APRICOT BALLS

8 ounces dried apricots
1 cup flaked coconut
¼ cup sweetened condensed milk
Additional flaked coconut for rolling (optional)

1. Chop apricots in food processor. Add coconut; process until combined. Add condensed milk; process until combined. Pour into pie pan. Refrigerate until firm enough to shape into balls, about 30 minutes.

2. Line baking sheet with buttered waxed paper; set aside.

3. Place additional coconut in shallow bowl.

4. Shape mixture into 1-inch balls. Roll in coconut. Place balls on prepared baking sheet. Refrigerate until firm. Store in refrigerator in airtight container.   *Makes about 22 balls*

DOUBLE CHOCOLATE TRUFFLES

½ cup whipping cream
1 tablespoon butter or margarine
4 bars (1 ounce each) HERSHEY'S Semi-Sweet Baking Chocolate, broken into pieces
1 HERSHEY'S Milk Chocolate Bar (7 ounces), broken into pieces
1 tablespoon amaretto (almond-flavored liqueur) *or* ¼ to ½ teaspoon almond extract
Ground almonds

In small saucepan, combine whipping cream and butter. Cook over medium heat, stirring constantly, just until mixture is very hot. Do not boil. Remove from heat; add chocolate, chocolate bar pieces and liqueur. Stir with whisk until smooth. Press plastic wrap directly onto surface; cool several hours or until mixture is firm enough to handle. Shape into 1-inch balls; roll in almonds to coat. Refrigerate until firm, about 2 hours. Store in tightly covered container in refrigerator.

Makes about 2 dozen candies

Top to bottom: Apricot Balls and Chocolate-Covered Raisins (page 347)

Coconut Bonbons

2 cups powdered sugar
3 tablespoons evaporated
   milk
2 tablespoons butter,
   softened
1 cup flaked coconut
1 teaspoon vanilla
1 cup (6 ounces) semisweet
   chocolate chips
1 tablespoon shortening

1. Line baking sheet with waxed paper; set aside.

2. Combine sugar, evaporated milk, butter, coconut and vanilla in medium bowl.

3. Shape sugar mixture into ½-inch balls; place on prepared baking sheet. Refrigerate until firm.

4. Melt chips with shortening in small saucepan over very low heat, stirring constantly.

5. Dip bonbons in melted chocolate. Remove excess chocolate by scraping bottom of bonbon across rim of saucepan; return to prepared baking sheet. Refrigerate until firm; store in refrigerator in airtight container.

Makes about 24 bonbons

Left to right: New Orleans Pralines (page 369), Lollipops (page 371), Simple Molded Candies (page 371) and Coconut Bonbons

335

Peanut Butter Truffles

2 cups (11½ ounces) milk
chocolate chips
½ cup whipping cream
2 tablespoons butter
½ cup creamy peanut butter
¾ cup finely chopped peanuts

1. Melt chips with whipping cream and butter in medium saucepan over low heat, stirring occasionally. Whisk in peanut butter until blended. Pour into pie pan. Refrigerate until mixture is fudgy, but soft, about 1 hour, stirring occasionally.

2. Shape about 1 tablespoonful of mixture into 1¼-inch ball. Repeat with remaining mixture. Place balls on waxed paper.

3. Place peanuts in shallow bowl. Roll balls in peanuts; place in small candy cups. (If coating mixture won't stick because truffle has set, roll between your palms until outside is soft.)

4. Truffles can be refrigerated 2 to 3 days or frozen several weeks. *Makes about 36 truffles*

Chocolate Fudge-Peanut Butter Balls

2 cups (11½ ounces) milk
chocolate chips
¼ cup half-and-half
⅓ cup creamy peanut butter
⅓ cup chopped peanuts

1. Melt chips with half-and-half in medium saucepan over low heat, stirring occasionally. Whisk in peanut butter until blended. Refrigerate until mixture is firm enough to shape into balls, but still soft, about 30 minutes, stirring occasionally.

2. Spread peanuts on waxed paper.

3. Shape mixture into 1-inch balls. Roll balls in peanuts. Store in refrigerator in airtight container. *Makes about 32 balls*

MARBLED TRUFFLES

6 ounces white chocolate, coarsely chopped
½ cup whipping cream, divided
1 teaspoon vanilla
1 cup (6 ounces) semisweet chocolate chips
1 tablespoon butter
2 tablespoons orange-flavored liqueur
¾ cup powdered sugar, sifted

1. Melt white chocolate with ¼ cup of the whipping cream and the vanilla in medium saucepan over low heat, stirring constantly. Pour into 9-inch square pan. Refrigerate.

2. Melt semisweet chocolate chips with butter and remaining ¼ cup whipping cream in medium saucepan over low heat, stirring constantly. Whisk in liqueur.

3. Pour chocolate mixture over refrigerated white chocolate mixture. Refrigerate until mixture is fudgy, but soft, about 1 hour.

4. Shape about 1 tablespoonful of the mixture into 1¼-inch ball. Repeat with remaining mixture. Place balls on waxed paper.

5. Sift powdered sugar into shallow bowl. Roll balls in powdered sugar; place in small candy cups. (If coating mixture won't stick because truffle has set, roll between your palms until outside is soft.) Truffles can be refrigerated 2 to 3 days or frozen several weeks.   *Makes about 30 truffles*

Hawaiian Toffee

HAWAIIAN TOFFEE

1 jar (3½ ounces) macadamia nuts (¾ cup), coarsely chopped
1 cup unsalted butter
1 cup sugar
2 tablespoons water
¼ teaspoon salt
1 teaspoon vanilla
4 ounces milk chocolate, chopped
1 cup flaked coconut, toasted

Hawaii's third largest crop, macadamia nuts are known for their buttery smooth flavor and delectable crunch. To retain freshness, store macadamia nuts in the refrigerator or freezer.

1. Line 9-inch square pan with heavy-duty foil, pressing foil into corners to cover completely and leaving 1-inch overhang on sides. Sprinkle nuts evenly in single layer in prepared pan.

2. Combine butter, sugar, water and salt in medium saucepan. Bring to a boil over medium heat, stirring frequently.

3. Attach candy thermometer to side of pan. (Bulb of thermometer should not rest on bottom of saucepan.) Continue boiling about 20 minutes or until sugar mixture reaches hard-crack stage (305° to 310°F) on candy thermometer, stirring frequently. Remove from heat; stir in vanilla. Immediately pour over nuts in pan. Cool completely, about 30 minutes.

4. Place chocolate in small microwavable bowl. Microwave at MEDIUM (50% power) 4 to 5 minutes until chocolate is melted, stirring every 2 minutes.

5. Remove toffee from pan. Spread chocolate evenly over toffee. Sprinkle with toasted coconut, pressing lightly with fingertips so coconut will adhere to chocolate. Refrigerate about 30 minutes or until chocolate is set. Bring to room temperature.

6. Break toffee into pieces. Store in airtight container at room temperature between sheets of waxed paper.

Makes about 1¼ pounds toffee

ALMOND BUTTER CRUNCH

1 cup **BLUE DIAMOND®**
    Blanched Slivered
    Almonds
½ **cup butter**
½ **cup sugar**
1 **tablespoon light corn syrup**

Line bottom and sides of 8- or 9-inch cake pan with aluminum foil (not plastic wrap or wax paper). Butter foil heavily; set aside. Combine almonds, butter, sugar and corn syrup in 10-inch skillet. Bring to a boil over medium heat, stirring constantly. Boil, stirring constantly, until mixture turns golden brown, about 5 to 6 minutes. Working quickly, spread candy in prepared pan. Cool about 15 minutes or until firm. Remove candy from pan by lifting edges of foil. Peel off foil. Cool thoroughly. Break into pieces. *Makes about ¾ pound*

CHOCOLATE BUTTER CRUNCH

1 **cup butter**
1¼ **cups sugar**
¼ **cup water**
2 **tablespoons light corn syrup**
1 **cup ground almonds,**
    divided
½ **teaspoon vanilla extract**
¾ **cup milk chocolate chips**

Line 15½×10½×1-inch jelly-roll pan with foil, extending edges over sides of pan. Generously grease foil.

Melt butter in medium saucepan over medium heat. Add sugar, water and corn syrup. Bring to a boil, stirring constantly.

Carefully clip candy thermometer to side of pan. (Do not let bulb touch bottom of pan.) Cook until thermometer registers 290°F, stirring frequently. Stir in ⅔ cup almonds and vanilla. Pour into prepared pan. Spread mixture into corners with metal spatula. Let stand 1 minute. Sprinkle with chocolate chips. Let stand 2 to 3 minutes more until chocolate melts. Spread chocolate over candy. Sprinkle with remaining ⅓ cup almonds. Cool completely.

Lift candy out of pan using foil; remove foil. Break candy into pieces. Store in airtight container.

Makes about 1½ pounds

Almond Butter Crunch

CASHEW MACADAMIA CRUNCH

2 cups (11.5 ounce package) HERSHEY'S Milk Chocolate Chips
¾ cup coarsely chopped salted or unsalted cashews
¾ cup coarsely chopped salted or unsalted macadamia nuts
½ cup (1 stick) butter, softened
½ cup sugar
2 tablespoons light corn syrup

1. Line 9-inch square pan with foil, extending foil over edges of pan. Butter foil. Cover bottom of prepared pan with chocolate chips.

2. Combine cashews, macadamia nuts, butter, sugar and corn syrup in large heavy skillet; cook over low heat, stirring constantly, until butter is melted and sugar is dissolved. Increase heat to medium; cook, stirring constantly, until mixture begins to cling together and turns golden brown.

3. Pour mixture over chocolate chips in pan, spreading evenly. Cool. Refrigerate until chocolate is firm. Remove from pan; peel off foil. Break into pieces. Store, tightly covered in cool, dry place. *Makes about 1½ pounds*

MICROWAVE NUT BRITTLE

MAZOLA NO STICK® Cooking Spray
1 cup sugar
½ cup KARO® Light Corn Syrup
⅛ teaspoon salt
1½ cups roasted peanuts, cashews or mixed nuts
1 teaspoon MAZOLA® Margarine or butter
1 teaspoon vanilla
1 teaspoon baking soda

1. Spray cookie sheet and metal spatula with cooking spray.

2. In 2-quart microwavable glass measuring cup or bowl, stir sugar, corn syrup and salt with wooden spoon until well mixed.

3. Microwave on High (100%) 7 to 8 minutes or until syrup is pale yellow. *(Candy syrup is very hot. Handle carefully; do not touch hot mixture.)* Stir in nuts.

4. Microwave on High 1 to 2 minutes or until nuts are lightly browned. Immediately stir in margarine, vanilla and baking soda until foamy.

5. Quickly pour onto cookie sheet; spread evenly with spatula. Cool; break into pieces. Store in tightly covered container. *Makes about 1¼ pounds*

Cashew Macadamia Crunch

CHOCOLATE-COATED ALMOND BRITTLE

1¾ cups sugar
⅓ cup KARO® Light Corn
   Syrup
¼ cup water
1 cup (2 sticks) MAZOLA®
   Margarine or butter
1½ cups finely chopped,
   toasted blanched
   almonds
Chocolate Glaze (recipe
   follows)
3 cups coarsely chopped,
   toasted blanched
   almonds, divided

1. In heavy 2-quart saucepan combine sugar, corn syrup and water. Stirring constantly, bring to boil over medium heat. Cover; cook 1 minute. Remove cover. Add margarine. Stirring constantly, cook until temperature on candy thermometer reaches 290°F or small amount of mixture dropped into very cold water separates into threads which are hard but not brittle. Remove from heat.

2. Quickly stir in 1½ cups almonds just until blended. Immediately pour into ungreased 15½×10½×1-inch baking pan, spreading quickly. Cool a few minutes until film forms on top.

3. Using wide metal spatula, mark surface into 1½-inch squares, beginning from outside, working toward center. Without breaking through film surface, press along marked lines. When spatula can be pressed to bottom of pan in all lines, candy is shaped. Cool.

4. Remove from pan and break into squares. Dip each square into Chocolate Glaze; coat with remaining chopped almonds. Place on waxed paper-lined tray. Refrigerate 20 to 25 minutes or until chocolate sets. Store in single layer in tightly covered container.   *Makes about 2 pounds*

CHOCOLATE GLAZE:

In 1-quart saucepan combine 3 squares (1 ounce each) semisweet chocolate, 3 squares (1 ounce each) unsweetened chocolate, ⅓ cup Mazola® Margarine or butter and 1½ tablespoons Karo® Light or Dark Corn Syrup. Stir over very low heat just until smooth. Remove from heat; beat with wooden spoon until cool but still pourable.

TRADITIONAL PEANUT BRITTLE

1½ cups salted peanuts
1 cup sugar
1 cup light corn syrup
¼ cup water
2 tablespoons butter
¼ teaspoon baking soda

Heavily butter large cookie sheet; set aside. Place peanuts in ungreased 8-inch square baking pan. To warm peanuts, place in oven and heat oven to 250°F.

Meanwhile, place sugar, corn syrup, water and butter in heavy 2-quart saucepan. Stir over medium-low heat until sugar has dissolved and mixture comes to a boil, being careful not to splash sugar mixture on side of pan. Carefully clip candy thermometer to side of pan. (Do not let bulb touch bottom of pan.) Cook over medium-low heat until thermometer registers 280°F, without stirring. Gradually stir in warm peanuts. Cook until thermometer registers 300°F (hard-crack stage), stirring frequently.

Immediately remove from heat; stir in baking soda until thoroughly blended. (Mixture will froth and foam.) Immediately pour onto prepared cookie sheet. Spread mixture evenly to form an even layer. Cool about 30 minutes or until set. Break brittle into pieces. Store in airtight container.

Makes about 1½ pounds candy

Tip: *Use almonds instead of peanuts and stir in ½ teaspoon almond extract with baking soda.*

Fudgy Banana Rocky Road Clusters

FUDGY BANANA ROCKY ROAD CLUSTERS

1 package (12 ounces) semisweet chocolate chips
⅓ cup peanut butter
3 cups miniature marshmallows
1 cup unsalted peanuts
1 cup banana chips

Line baking sheets with buttered waxed paper; set aside.

Place chocolate chips and peanut butter in large microwavable bowl. Microwave at HIGH 2 minutes or until chips are melted and mixture is smooth, stirring twice. Fold in marshmallows, peanuts and banana chips.

Drop rounded tablespoonfuls candy mixture onto prepared baking sheets; refrigerate until firm. Store in airtight container in refrigerator. *Makes 2½ to 3 dozen clusters*

RAISIN CLUSTERS

1 cup milk chocolate chips
⅓ cup sweetened condensed milk
1 teaspoon vanilla
2 cups raisins

Line baking sheet with buttered waxed paper; set aside.

Melt chocolate with condensed milk and vanilla in small saucepan over low heat, stirring occasionally. Remove from heat. Stir in raisins. Drop by teaspoonfuls onto prepared baking sheet. Refrigerate until firm.

Store in refrigerator in airtight container between layers of waxed paper. *Makes 30 clusters*

CHOCOLATE-COVERED RAISINS

2 cups (11½ ounces) milk chocolate chips
1 square (1 ounce) unsweetened chocolate, chopped
1 tablespoon shortening
2 cups raisins

Line baking sheet with buttered waxed paper; set aside.

Melt chips and chopped chocolate with shortening in medium saucepan over low heat, stirring constantly. Stir in raisins. Drop individual raisins or drop in clusters from spoon onto prepared baking sheet. Let stand until firm.

Makes about 1½ pounds

PEANUT BUTTER CEREAL TREATS

**MAZOLA NO STICK®
Cooking Spray
4 cups crispy rice cereal or
combination of ready-to-
eat cereals***
**½ cup KARO® Light or Dark
Corn Syrup**
½ cup sugar
**½ cup SKIPPY® SUPER
CHUNK® or creamy
peanut butter**

**If using flake cereal, increase
amount to 5 cups.*

1. Spray 8- or 9-inch square baking pan with cooking spray. Pour cereal into large bowl.

2. In medium saucepan combine corn syrup and sugar. Stirring occasionally, bring to boil over medium heat and boil 1 minute. Remove from heat.

3. Stir in peanut butter until smooth. Pour over cereal; stir to coat well.

4. Press evenly into prepared pan. Cool about 15 minutes. Invert onto cutting board. Cut into 1½-inch bars.

Makes 36 bars

Microwave Directions: *Prepare pan as directed above. In 2-quart microwavable bowl combine corn syrup, sugar and peanut butter. Microwave on High (100%), stirring twice, 3½ to 4 minutes or until mixture is smooth and sugar is dissolved. Continue as above in steps 3 and 4.*

S'mores Treats: *Prepare Peanut Butter Cereal Treats as above; do not remove from pan. Melt 1 package (11½ ounces) milk chocolate chips; spread over top. Sprinkle with 2 cups miniature marshmallows. Broil a few seconds, just until golden brown. Cool.*

Peanut Butter Cereal Treats

CHOCOLATE-GRANOLA BARS

3 cups raisin-and-nut granola
½ cup finely chopped dried apricots
½ cup finely chopped dates
12 ounces white chocolate, coarsely chopped
¼ cup half-and-half or evaporated milk

1. Butter 8-inch square pan. Combine granola, apricots and dates in medium heat-proof bowl; set aside.

2. Melt white chocolate with half-and-half in small pan over low heat, stirring constantly.

3. Pour chocolate mixture over granola mixture and stir until coated. Press into prepared pan. Refrigerate until firm.

4. Cut into 2×1-inch bars. Store in refrigerator.

Makes 32 bars

YOGURT-RAISIN BARS

2 cups white chocolate, coarsely chopped
¼ cup plain yogurt, room temperature
1 teaspoon vanilla
2½ cups golden or dark raisins

1. Line 8-inch square pan with buttered foil; set aside.

2. Place white chocolate in small microwavable bowl. Microwave on MEDIUM 2 minutes, stirring after every minute. Stir until smooth. If not completely melted, microwave on MEDIUM 30 seconds more.

3. Stir in yogurt and vanilla until smooth. Stir in raisins. Press into prepared pan. Refrigerate until set.

4. Remove candy from pan by lifting out foil. Cut into 2×1-inch bars. Store in refrigerator. *Makes 32 bars*

Fruit Bars

1 cup chopped figs
1 cup chopped dates
1 cup chopped dried pears
1 cup finely chopped pecans
¼ cup orange marmalade

1. Butter 8-inch square pan; set aside.

2. Combine all ingredients in medium bowl. Press mixture in prepared pan. Refrigerate until set.

3. Cut into bars. Store in refrigerator.   *Makes 32 bars*

Hint: *To prepare without a food processor, finely chop fruit and nuts. Combine fruit and nuts in medium bowl. Stir in marmalade.*

Toasted Almond Bark

½ cup slivered almonds
12 ounces white chocolate, coarsely chopped
1 tablespoon shortening

1. Preheat oven to 325°F.

2. Spread almonds on baking sheet. Bake 12 minutes or until golden brown, stirring occasionally.

3. Meanwhile, butter another baking sheet. Spread warm almonds on buttered baking sheet.

4. Melt white chocolate with shortening in small saucepan over very low heat, stirring constantly.

5. Spoon evenly over almonds, spreading about ¼ inch thick. Refrigerate until almost firm.

6. Cut into squares, but do not remove from baking sheet. Refrigerate until firm.   *Makes about 1 pound*

CARAMEL-NUT CHOCOLATE CUPS

36 Chocolate Cups (recipe on page 314) or purchased chocolate liqueur cups
¾ cup plus 36 pecan halves, divided
¾ cup caramel-flavored topping
1⅛ cups semisweet chocolate chips
1½ teaspoons vegetable shortening

1. Prepare Chocolate Cups; set aside.

2. Preheat oven to 375°F. Spread pecans on baking sheet. Bake 8 to 10 minutes or until golden brown, stirring frequently. Remove from baking sheet; cool. Chop ¾ cup pecan halves into uniform pieces. Reserve 36 pecan halves.

3. Spoon 1 teaspoon caramel topping into each Chocolate Cup. Top each with 1 teaspoon chopped pecans, pressing gently; set aside.

4. Place chocolate and shortening in top of double boiler over simmering water. Stir until chocolate is melted. Remove from heat.

5. Spoon 1 teaspoon melted chocolate around perimeter of each cup. Immediately place one toasted pecan half in center. Let stand in cool place until firm. Store at room temperature in airtight container.

Makes 36 Caramel-Nut Chocolate Cups

Caramel-Nut Chocolate Cups

353

Peanut Butter Cups

2 cups (12 ounces) semisweet
chocolate chips
1 cup (6 ounces) milk
chocolate chips
1½ cups confectioners' sugar
1 cup crunchy or smooth
peanut butter
½ cup vanilla wafer crumbs
(about 11 wafers)
6 tablespoons butter,
softened

Line 12 (2½-inch) muffin cups with double-thickness paper cups or foil cups; set aside. Melt both chips in small saucepan over very low heat, stirring constantly.

Spoon about 1 tablespoonful of the chocolate into each cup. With back of spoon, bring chocolate up side of each cup. Refrigerate until firm, about 20 minutes.

Combine sugar, peanut butter, crumbs and butter in medium bowl. Spoon 2 tablespoons of the peanut butter mixture into each chocolate cup. Spread with small spatula. Spoon about 1 tablespoon remaining chocolate over each peanut butter cup. Refrigerate until firm. *Makes 12 cups*

Marshmallow Cups

2 cups (11½ ounces) milk
chocolate chips
2 tablespoons shortening
1 cup (½ of 7-ounce jar)
marshmallow creme

1. Line 18 mini-muffin cups with double-thickness paper cups or foil cups; set aside. Melt chips with shortening in small saucepan over very low heat, stirring constantly.

2. Spoon about ½ tablespoonful of the chocolate mixture into each cup. With back of spoon, bring chocolate up side of each cup.

3. Spoon 1 tablespoonful of the marshmallow creme into each chocolate cup, using spoons dipped in hot water. Spread with small spatula.

4. Spoon about ½ tablespoonful of remaining chocolate over each marshmallow cup. Refrigerate until firm. *Makes 18 cups*

CREAMY CHOCOLATE DIPPED STRAWBERRIES

1 cup HERSHEY'S Semi-Sweet Chocolate Chips
½ cup HERSHEY'S Premier White Chips
1 tablespoon shortening (do not use butter, margarine or oil)
Fresh strawberries, rinsed and patted dry (about 2 pints)

Line tray with wax paper. In medium microwave-safe bowl, place chocolate chips, white chips and shortening. Microwave at HIGH (100%) 1 minute; stir. If necessary, microwave at HIGH an additional 15 seconds at a time, stirring after each heating, just until chips are melted when stirred. Holding top, dip bottom two-thirds of each strawberry into melted mixture; shake gently to remove excess. Place on prepared tray. Refrigerate about 1 hour or until coating is firm. Cover; refrigerate leftover dipped berries. For best results, use within 24 hours.

Makes about 3 dozen dipped berries

CHOCOLATE-DIPPED DELIGHTS

Assorted fruit, nuts or pretzels
4 squares BAKER'S® Semi-Sweet Chocolate, melted
Colored sprinkles (optional)

INSERT long wooden picks into fruit to be dipped. Dip fruit, nuts or pretzels into chocolate, covering at least half; let excess chocolate drip off. Sprinkle with colored sprinkles, if desired. Let stand or refrigerate on wire rack or waxed paper-lined tray until chocolate is firm, about 30 minutes. Store in refrigerator up to 2 days. *Makes about 2 dozen candies*

DOUBLE DIPPED APPLES

MAZOLA NO STICK®
Cooking Spray
5 medium apples
5 wooden sticks
1 package (14 ounces)
caramel candies,
unwrapped
¼ cup KARO® Light or Dark
Corn Syrup
¾ cup chopped walnuts
1 cup (6 ounces) semisweet
chocolate chips
1 teaspoon MAZOLA® Corn
Oil

1. Spray small cookie sheet with cooking spray; set aside. Wash and dry apples; insert stick into stem end.

2. In small, deep microwavable bowl microwave caramels and corn syrup at HIGH 3 to 4 minutes or until caramels are melted and smooth, stirring after each minute.

3. Dip apples in hot caramel mixture, turning to coat well. Allow caramel to drip from apples for a few seconds, then scrape excess from bottom of apples. Roll bottom half in walnuts. Place on prepared cookie sheet. Refrigerate at least 15 minutes.

4. In small microwavable bowl, microwave chocolate and corn oil at HIGH 1 to 2 minutes; stir until melted.

5. Drizzle apples with chocolate. Refrigerate 10 minutes or until chocolate is firm. Wrap apples individually; store in refrigerator.   *Makes 5 apples*

Double Dipped Apples

BLACK AND WHITE CARAMELS

CARAMELS
>2 cups sugar
>2 cups light corn syrup
>1 cup half-and-half
>1 cup unsalted butter
>½ teaspoon salt
>1 cup whipping cream
>1 teaspoon vanilla

COATING
>12 ounces semisweet
>>chocolate, chopped
>14 to 16 ounces white
>>chocolate, chopped and
>>divided
>6 teaspoons shortening

1. To prepare caramels, line 8-inch square pan with heavy-duty foil, pressing foil into corners to cover completely and leaving 1-inch overhang on sides. Lightly butter foil.

2. Combine sugar, corn syrup, half-and-half, butter and salt in large saucepan. Bring to a boil over medium-high heat, stirring occasionally. Wash down sugar crystals with pastry brush, if necessary. Carefully clip candy thermometer to side of pan. (Do not let bulb touch bottom of pan.) Continue boiling 25 minutes or until sugar mixture reaches firm-ball stage (244° to 246°F) on candy thermometer, stirring frequently. Remove from heat; very gradually stir in cream.

3. Return to medium heat. Cook 15 minutes or until mixture reaches 248°F on candy thermometer, stirring frequently. Remove from heat; stir in vanilla. Immediately pour into prepared pan. (Do not scrape saucepan.) Cool at room temperature 3 to 4 hours until firm.

4. Remove from pan by lifting caramels using foil handles. Place on cutting board; peel off foil. Cut into 1-inch strips. Cut each strip into 1-inch squares with buttered knife. Line two 13×9-inch baking pans with waxed paper; lightly butter paper. Place squares into prepared pans spacing each ¾ inch apart. Cover tightly with plastic wrap and let stand overnight at room temperature.

5. To prepare coating, temper semisweet chocolate according to directions on page 7. Lower caramels into tempered chocolate with dipping fork or spoon (do not pierce), tapping handle gently against side of pan to allow

continued on page 360

Black and White Caramels

Black and White Caramels, continued from page 358

excess chocolate to drain back into pan. Remove excess chocolate by scraping bottom of caramel across rim of saucepan.

6. Place caramels on waxed paper. Let stand in cool place until chocolate is firm. (Do not refrigerate.)

7. Place 12 ounces of white chocolate and all of shortening in a clean double boiler; temper according to directions on page 7. Dip remaining caramels as directed in Step 5. As soon as white chocolate starts to thicken too much, return top pan to double boiler momentarily; stir in 1 additional ounce of white chocolate until mixture loosens without exceeding recommended temperature. Continue dipping, adding remaining white chocolate as needed periodically, until all caramels are coated.

8. Store coated caramels in airtight container at room temperature.

Makes 64 chocolate coated 1-inch caramels

WHITE CHOCOLATE-DIPPED APRICOTS

3 ounces white chocolate, coarsely chopped
20 dried apricot halves

Line baking sheet with waxed paper; set aside. Melt white chocolate in bowl over hot (not boiling) water; stir constantly.

Dip half of each apricot piece in chocolate, coating both sides. Place on prepared baking sheet. Refrigerate until firm. Store in refrigerator in container between layers of waxed paper.

Makes 20 apricots

White Chocolate-Dipped Apricots and Stuffed Pecans (page 368)

PECAN ROLLS

¼ cup corn syrup
¼ cup water
1¼ cups sugar
1 egg white
⅛ teaspoon cream of tartar
1 teaspoon vanilla
1 package (14 ounces)
    caramels
3 tablespoons water
2 cups coarsely chopped
    pecans

Line 9×5-inch loaf pan with buttered waxed paper; set aside. Combine corn syrup, water and sugar in small saucepan. Cook over medium heat, stirring constantly, until sugar dissolves and mixture comes to a boil. Wash down side of pan frequently with pastry brush dipped in hot water to remove sugar crystals. Carefully clip candy thermometer to side of pan. (Do not let bulb touch bottom of pan.) Continue to cook until mixture reaches the hard-ball stage (255°F).

Meanwhile, beat egg white and cream of tartar with electric mixer until stiff but not dry. Slowly pour hot syrup into egg white mixture, beating constantly. Add vanilla; beat until candy forms soft peaks and starts to lose its gloss. Spoon mixture into prepared pan. Cut into 3 strips lengthwise, then crosswise in center. Freeze until firm.

Line baking sheet with waxed paper; set aside. Melt caramels with water in small saucepan over low heat, stirring occasionally. Arrange pecans on waxed paper. Working quickly, drop 1 piece of frozen candy mixture into melted caramels to coat. Roll in pecans to coat completely. Place on prepared baking sheet to set. Repeat with remaining candy pieces, reheating caramels if mixture becomes too thick.

Cut logs into ½-inch slices. Store in refrigerator in airtight container between layers of waxed paper or freeze up to 3 months. *Makes 6 (5-inch) rolls*

Hint: For perfect slices, freeze finished rolls before cutting.

Pecan Rolls

DIVINITY

2½ cups sugar
½ cup KARO® Light Corn
      Syrup
½ cup water
¼ teaspoon salt
2 egg whites, at room
      temperature
1 teaspoon vanilla
1 cup chopped nuts (optional)

1. In 2-quart saucepan combine sugar, corn syrup, water and salt. Stirring constantly, bring to boil over medium heat. Without stirring, cook over low heat (small to medium bubbles breaking across surface of liquid) until temperature on candy thermometer reaches 266°F or small amount of mixture dropped into very cold water forms a hard ball which doesn't flatten until pressed, about 40 minutes.

2. When temperature reaches 260°F, in large bowl with mixer at high speed, beat egg whites until stiff peaks form. Beating at high speed, gradually add hot syrup in a thin steady stream. DO NOT SCRAPE MIXTURE FROM SIDE OF SAUCEPAN INTO BOWL. Continue beating at high speed until mixture begins to lose its gloss, about 3 minutes.

3. Reduce speed to low. Beat in vanilla. Continue beating at low speed until mixture holds a peak and does not spread when dropped from a spoon, about 8 minutes. (If mixture becomes too stiff for mixer, beat with wooden spoon.) Immediately stir in nuts.

4. Working quickly, drop by teaspoonfuls onto waxed paper.* If desired, garnish with walnut pieces or candied cherries. Let stand until set. Store in tightly covered container.

Makes about 1¼ pounds

Or, spread in 8- or 9-inch square baking pan lined with plastic wrap. If desired, garnish with walnut pieces or candied cherries. Cool on wire rack. Cut into squares. Store in tightly covered container.

Note: To color Divinity, add few drops food color with vanilla.

Peppermint Divinity: Line 8- or 9-inch square baking pan with plastic wrap. Follow recipe for Divinity. Omit nuts. Immediately after beating, fold in ¼ cup crushed peppermint candy. Pour into prepared pan. Cool on wire rack. Cut into squares.

Peanut Butter Divinity: Follow recipe for Divinity. Omit nuts. Immediately after beating, add ⅓ cup Skippy Super Chunk or creamy peanut butter; fold just until marbleized.

Dried Cherry or Cranberry Divinity: Follow recipe for Divinity. Omit nuts. Immediately after beating, fold in 1 cup chopped dried cherries or cranberries.

Butterscotch-Chocolate Divinity

2 cups sugar
⅓ cup light corn syrup
⅓ cup water
2 egg whites
⅛ teaspoon cream of tartar
1 teaspoon vanilla
½ cup milk chocolate chips
½ cup butterscotch chips
½ cup chopped nuts

Line 2 or 3 baking sheets with buttered waxed paper; set aside. Combine sugar, corn syrup and water in medium saucepan. Cook over medium heat, stirring constantly, until sugar dissolves and mixture comes to a boil. Wash down side of pan frequently with pastry brush dipped in hot water to remove sugar crystals. Add candy thermometer. (Do not let bulb touch bottom of pan.) Continue to cook until mixture reaches the hard-ball stage (255°F).

Meanwhile, beat egg whites and cream of tartar with electric mixer until stiff but not dry. Slowly pour hot syrup into egg whites, beating constantly. Add vanilla; beat until candy forms soft peaks and starts to lose its gloss. Stir in both kinds of chips and nuts. Immediately drop tablespoonfuls of candy in mounds on prepared baking sheets. Store in refrigerator in airtight container between layers of waxed paper or freeze up to 3 months. *Makes about 36 pieces*

Butterscotch-Chocolate Divinity

STUFFED PECANS

½ cup semisweet chocolate
  chips
¼ cup sweetened condensed
  milk
½ teaspoon vanilla
  Powdered sugar (about
  ½ cup)
80 large pecan halves

Melt chips in very small saucepan over very low heat, stirring constantly. Remove from heat. Stir in condensed milk and vanilla until smooth. Stir in enough sugar to make stiff mixture. Refrigerate, if needed.

Place 1 rounded teaspoonful chocolate mixture on flat side of 1 pecan half. Top with another pecan half. Repeat with remaining pecans and chocolate mixture. Store in refrigerator.

Makes about 40 candies

CHERRY-CHOCOLATE LOGS

1 cup (6 ounces) semisweet
  chocolate chips
¼ cup sweetened condensed
  milk
¼ teaspoon almond extract
½ cup quartered maraschino
  cherries, drained
1 cup coarsely chopped
  pecans

1. Melt chips in heavy saucepan over very low heat, stirring constantly. Stir in condensed milk and almond extract. Remove from heat.

2. Stir in cherries. Refrigerate until mixture can be shaped into logs, about 15 minutes.

3. Shape into 2 (1½-inch) logs. Roll logs in pecans. Refrigerate until firm.

4. Cut into ½-inch slices. Store in refrigerator.

Makes about ¾ pound

New Orleans Pralines

1 cup packed brown sugar
½ cup granulated sugar
½ cup heavy or whipping
   cream
¼ cup **KARO®** Light Corn
   Syrup
1 tablespoon **MAZOLA®**
   Margarine or butter
1 teaspoon vanilla
1½ cups coarsely broken pecans

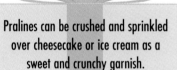

Pralines can be crushed and sprinkled over cheesecake or ice cream as a sweet and crunchy garnish.

1. Line large cookie sheets with waxed paper.

2. In 3-quart saucepan combine brown sugar, granulated sugar, cream and corn syrup. Stirring frequently, bring to boil over medium-low heat. Reduce heat to low. Stirring frequently, cook until temperature reaches 238°F on candy thermometer or until small amount of mixture dropped into very cold water forms a soft ball which flattens on removal.

3. Remove from heat. Add margarine and vanilla. With wooden spoon beat 1 to 2 minutes or until mixture begins to thicken and looks opaque. Stir in pecans until well coated.

4. Working quickly, drop mixture by tablespoonfuls onto prepared cookie sheets. When cool, remove from paper. Store in airtight container with waxed paper between layers.

Makes about 24 (3-inch) pralines

369

ELEGANT CREAM CHEESE MINTS

Chocolate Topping (recipe follows), optional

1 package (3 ounces) cream cheese, softened

3 tablespoons butter, softened

½ teaspoon vanilla extract

¼ to ½ teaspoon desired food coloring

¼ teaspoon peppermint extract

1 pound powdered sugar (3½ to 4 cups)

⅓ cup granulated sugar

Line large cookie sheet with waxed paper. Prepare Chocolate Topping, if desired; keep warm.

Beat cream cheese, butter, vanilla, food coloring and peppermint extract in large bowl with electric mixer on medium speed until smooth. Gradually beat in powdered sugar on low speed until well combined. (If necessary, stir in remaining powdered sugar with wooden spoon or knead candy on work surface sprinkled lightly with powdered sugar.)

Place granulated sugar in shallow bowl. Roll 2 teaspoons of cream cheese mixture into a ball. Roll ball in granulated sugar until coated. Flatten ball with fingers or fork to make a patty. Place patty on prepared cookie sheet. Repeat with remaining cream cheese mixture and sugar. Drizzle patties with topping, if desired. Refrigerate until firm. Store in airtight container in refrigerator.   *Makes about 1½ pounds or 40 (1-inch) mints*

CHOCOLATE TOPPING:

Place ½ cup semisweet chocolate chips and 1 tablespoon shortening in 1-cup glass measuring cup. Microwave on HIGH (100%) about 2 minutes or until melted, stirring after 1½ minutes.

Lollipops

1 cup water
²/₃ cup corn syrup
2 cups sugar
½ teaspoon oil of cinnamon, peppermint, anise or cloves
Food coloring

Oil lollipop mold and place lollipop sticks in position or butter 2 baking sheets; set aside.

Combine water, corn syrup and sugar in medium saucepan. Cook over medium heat, stirring constantly, until sugar dissolves and mixture comes to a boil. Wash down side of pan with pastry brush frequently dipped in hot water to remove sugar crystals. Carefully clip candy thermometer to side of pan. (Do not let bulb touch bottom of pan.) Continue to cook until mixture reaches the hard-crack stage (300°F). Remove from heat.

Add oil of cinnamon. Add food coloring, a few drops at a time, until desired color is obtained. Spoon hot mixture into prepared molds, making sure top of sticks are covered with syrup. Or, spread on prepared baking sheets and score into squares while still slightly warm. Unmold lollipops or break squares into pieces when firm.   *Makes about 1½ pounds*

Simple, Molded Candy

12 ounces confectioner's coating
Food coloring (optional)

1. Melt confectioner's coating in bowl over hot, not boiling water, stirring constantly. Add food coloring, a few drops at a time, until desired color is obtained.

2. Spoon into molds. Tap molds on countertop to remove bubbles. Refrigerate until firm. Bring to room temperature before unmolding to avoid cracking molds.

Makes about 24 candies

ACKNOWLEDGMENTS

The publisher would like to thank the companies and organizations listed below for the use of their recipes and photographs in this publication.

Best Foods

Blue Diamond Growers®

Bob Evans®

California Prune Board

Del Monte Corporation

Domino Sugar Corporation

Equal® sweetener

Hershey Foods Corporation

Kahlúa® Liqueur

Kraft Foods, Inc.

M&M/MARS

McIlhenny Company (TABASCO® Pepper Sauce)

MOTT'S® Inc., a division of Cadbury Beverages Inc.

National Honey Board

National Sunflower Association

Nestlé USA, Inc.

The Procter & Gamble Company

The Quaker® Kitchens

Reckitt & Colman Inc.

The Sugar Association, Inc.

Walnut Marketing Board

Washington Apple Commission

Wisconsin Milk Marketing Board

C

INDEX